90 Days of Love

90 Days of Love

Chris Enni

Mastering love to create your fulfilling life!

ISBN-13: 978-1-7342457-0-7

Published by Partnership and Love
info@partnershipandlove.com
www.partnershipandlove.com
https://www.facebook.com/partnershipandlove/

Inside Cover photo by Freestocks.org

Dedicated to Sarah and our respective children:
Bella and Domaso; Danielle and Derek.
May you master love for your own fulfilling life.

Table of Contents

About Love

Introduction

Are you struggling with closeness and intimacy? Are your relationships anything but smooth and easy? Do you often hide things about yourself, or feel fear, guilt, shame, disappointment, resentment? Do you imagine that your relationships can be happier, healthier, full of love and joy?

Good news! No matter where you are in your relationships, you can create closeness and intimacy. No matter where you are in your life, you can feel love. No matter what has happened to you, you can create a life of love.

So yes! You have found a book that will let you in on the secrets of love. Though it is not until you experience these 90 exercises that you will understand them. Love is important, just as you are important.

What's at stake is the full potential of love that you are capable of feeling everyday. What's at stake is the loving home, family, community and world that we all have dreamed. What's at stake is you living the best life available to you—a life fueled by love.

Imagine having a lover who knows everything about you, accepts you, encourages you, and thinks you are the best thing to have ever happened. I know this is possible because this is how my partner and I are with each other. We aren't lucky. We do these exercises, not for practice, but for real life, which like yours, is full of problems to solve and overcome. We approach our life together with great love for each other, our family, and all people. This makes the difference between a normal relationship and an extraordinary partnership.

Begin your journey today, stay on course, and you will arrive at your intended destination. I am sharing these exercises with you because they work. I want you to create the greatest relationship of your life, romantic or otherwise, just as I have done.

My recommendation is that you get started on the exercises while reading this About Love section. I suggest this because it's the exercises that will improve your love life, not the explanations. Reading about lifting weights does not grow muscle. Repeatedly lifting weights does. There's no other way around, over, or under, becoming a Master of Love. The only way is through the journey, and it is worth the effort.

Plan to create time in the morning to read the exercises. Or read them the night before to get ready for the next day. Experiencing an increase in love, whether for one person or many people, is a victory. And what a sweet victory it is when you achieve a life of love!

90 Days of Love is about taking action and making progress. It is not about perfection or doing things right. If you get behind, that's OK. Get caught back up. Even doing at least two per week can work. Just keep moving. The exercises are designed to ease you into the work. If you find that the early exercises are too easy, then by all means, skip ahead to the ones that dig deep. More of the later exercises take on real life issues and situations.

I also suggest that whether you do all of the exercises or not, read the entire book. This will tune your mind and heart to the practice of love and help you find your own path.

You will need to work on some exercises more than others. Find the ones that expand your love and practice those over and over. Love is not a 1-day, 7-day, or 90-day endeavor, but a life-long commitment.

My Story

At a young age, I noticed that for some, love was easy. That was never the case for me. Falling in love was easy. The relationship was hard and when it ended, I felt worse about myself. I just could not make it work.

My childhood had been fraught with heartache, anger and fear. My parents divorced when I was young. Within months, my mother remarried and I belonged to a new family in a new city. Overwhelmed, I buried my emotions, stuffing far down inside of myself the pain and sadness of loss. For the next forty years, I remained in that state, even through periods of dating, marriage, parenthood and career. I never felt happy, always feeling like something was missing.

In my mid-forties, I struck up a friendly relationship with a woman with whom I began to share my inner thoughts. Soon, I began to have feelings that I had never had before. "Was this love?" I asked myself. My only conclusion was that it was love, and that for over four decades, I had never known what love felt like. Because of my inexperience with love, connection and vulnerability, I didn't know how to conduct myself in that relationship and like all of the others, it ended in devastating disaster.

My entire life, I had been missing an intimate connection with another human being—love. I had only a faint glimmer of it. When I finally opened myself up to another person, love came pouring out, so much so that it hurt. I remember having spasms of pain shoot throughout my body as I thought about her. "What's going on?" I asked myself. I thought I was going crazy, but later I realized that the great amount of love within me could only express itself through my dilapidated "love center." Because of lack of use, it had become decrepit and fallen to pieces. I knew, to have the relationship of my dreams, I had to fix it. At that moment in my life, I vowed to discover the secrets to love and recreate that feeling inside of me.

The growth of love in my life began with reading books, taking relationship courses, and practicing with family. I made many mistakes and often failed, falling back into pain, anger, sadness and fear. I continued to have difficulty conversing with people, but continued doing every exercise I could find. Eventually I began to make friends. I even began to create my own love exercises. The feeling that I had thought was love began to come back, stronger and healthier than before.

Now I am in my early fifties and I have created the greatest romantic relationship of my life with no indication of any upper limit to the amount of love I feel for her. And she loves all of me, including those parts of myself that I always wanted to hide from others. I credit these exercises, along with the principles of partnership, for this success.

The most effective exercises I did always involved moving toward and through my pain, fears and any uncomfortable emotions. Whenever I attempted to avoid these, my life and relationships grew worse. On the other hand, every time I conquered an exercise that brought up pain, fear and uncomfortableness, I became emotionally stronger and empowered myself to take on my dreams, many of them coming true. My romantic relationship is a dream come true. This book is a dream come true, as well.

The Three Laws of Love

90 Days of Love, first and foremost, is based on the following Three Laws of Love. As you go through the exercises, you will begin to see these laws in action.

1. *Your ability to love is proportional to the robustness of your love center, that part of yourself that gives and receives love.*

   Human beings are highly adaptable. As you increase the experiences of love in your life, your mind, body and spirit will grow your love center. You can and will adapt yourself into a loving person.

2. *You cannot control anyone other than yourself.*

   You cannot make anyone love you. All you can do is make yourself a loving person. Love encompasses letting go of control. This leads to the third law:

3. *You can only have a loving relationship with another person who chooses to have a loving relationship with you.*

   Not everyone is available for love. Each person has their own journey to make in opening up to love. But by opening yourself up to love as fully as possible, you can influence and inspire others to make this journey with you.

The Five Secrets of Love

From the Three Laws of Love, and through my own practices and understanding, I have become aware of The Five Secrets of Love. I call them secrets because many people do not know about them. But the real secret is that great love has been inside of you the entire time.

LOVE SECRET #1

You are capable of realizing your dreams of love

You are a normal and whole human being, fully capable of living a life of love and creating a #10 relationship.

90 Days of Love is about exercising and strengthening your love center, not only by educating you about love, but also by giving you easy exercises to experience the great power of love inside of you. To attract more love into your life, you must first BE a loving person.

Love is a higher form of survival that compels you to want to be with others and live in harmony. Love, when robustly integrated in your core, will establish control over your fight or flight reactions, and over your feelings of fear, anger and hate. Moreover, because love emanates from the newest parts of your brain, and these parts can be re-wired, renewed, and regrown, you have the ability to learn to love.

You can learn to love! I know because I have greatly increased my own love center.

LOVE SECRET #2

Love is the emotion of connection

When you think of the love you want, what you are really thinking is that you want the experience of connecting with another human being. Connection is the universal link between all people. You experience this universal link at different levels such as the spiritual, emotional, mental, and physical levels. When you have an experience of connection, you feel love.

To reiterate, love begins in the newest parts of the brain, whereas fear and anger find their source in the primitive parts of the brain. If you were loved supremely by your mother and father, cared for by your family, and generally experienced a loving childhood, your love center was activated and strengthened. When you have a connected childhood, you can easily love and be resilient in adulthood.

But when you have a disconnected childhood, knowing how to connect with another human being can be like communicating with someone in a foreign language. Without the lessons of connection from your caregivers, your primitive brain's fear, anger, and other instincts for survival can overwhelm or overpower your love center. This can suffocate your natural ability to love in the long-term.

Fortunately, the ability to learn love never goes away. If you want stronger muscles, you exercise and lift weights every day to make those muscles bigger. If you have never exercised before, it would take a long time to achieve a muscular body. But here's the key fact. You already have muscles. Barring a terrible disease, your muscles never disappear. They are always there, ready to start exercising.

The same with the love center in your brain and body. It's always there, waiting to be activated. That's why I came up with these love exercises. They will activate your ability to connect with yourself and with people, thus producing the experience of love.

LOVE SECRET #3

You are able to consciously create love

You have the ability to control the amount of love you give and receive. The amount of love you have is not dependent on your past, or who you are. The amount of love you have is dependent on whether your love center is activated and used. The more you use it, the more love you will have in your life.

Since love is an experience of connection, by creating such an experience, you will create the feeling of love. Adversely, and please pay attention here, by creating experiences of disconnection with people, you will diminish love. *90 Days of Love* is designed for you to experience connection with people, nature and the most important person in the world, you.

Directing yourself to love may not be in your playbook, so you may take this secret with a grain of salt. Allow me to tell you that you are always creating experiences of connection and disconnection with other people. It's just a matter of making you aware of your own power to create connections and land it squarely in the commanding portion of your mind. You can choose to love yourself, one other person, all people, or a number in-between. You can also choose to receive love from yourself, one other person, all people, or a number in-between. It's all your choice. It is up to you.

LOVE SECRET #4

Your thoughts and behaviors affect your love

Two things trigger feelings: thoughts and behaviors. Since the nervous system is the source of your feelings, and you possess consciousness, or the ability to self-direct, then your conscious thoughts can trigger feelings of love by either thinking about love or performing acts of love. Therefore it is vitally important for the success of your love life to specifically conjure all of your thoughts toward love and connection.

Your feelings pull the knobs and levers of your behaviors, much like a crane operator maneuvers tons of cargo with minimal effort. Put simply, you do what you feel. This means that your feelings and behaviors are interconnected. So it stands to reason that the effect can run in reverse. That is, your behaviors will influence your feelings. There are wise sayings to this truth such as "Fake it 'til you make it!" or "If you want to feel better, smile," meaning that if you change your behavior, you will change your feelings. Try it out for yourself.

Some people think that the only working method of controlling behaviors is by suppressing feelings. Though it does work, it is very inefficient because it takes energy to suppress what is natural. In the end, suppressing your feelings only diminishes the human experience rather than enhancing it.

Plainly put: think love, act loving, and you will feel love.

LOVE SECRET #5

The more you connect with people, the more they will connect with you

An amazing thing begins to happen as you open yourself up to people. They begin to open up to you. By allowing other people to get to know all of you: good, bad, ups, downs, successes, failures, shallowness and depths, you give them permission to reveal themselves to you. And they do! Not everyone, but many.

If someone doesn't connect with you, it's most likely because they are protecting their broken heart. As you begin to love others, you will find some of them resistant to being loved, just as I was at one point.

Let's assume there are three kinds of broken-hearted people. The first are the kind that never learned to love and so connection is unfamiliar and uncomfortable territory. The second kind are those that once loved, but because they experienced loss, betrayal, rejection, control or anything else that can cause emotional pain, they now fear connection. Finally there are the third kind that fall in love for the thrills and not for connection.

If you are one of these kinds of broken-hearted people, this last secret is for you (as it was for me). Your revitalization can come from two directions. The first direction is from outside of yourself. Someone will love you so much that you will begin to experience connection and begin the process of learning to love. Though most likely you will put up a battle, resist connection, and defend your reality of separateness. Have you ever had the experience of someone loving you and still feeling uncomfortable, possibly giving them the "Goodbye" even when things were good?

The second direction is from within yourself. This will come from putting time and energy into you, working on you, and practicing love. I promise, creating the love that you want is easier and more rewarding than waiting for the love that you want. You will give yourself the opportunity to make the uncomfortable comfortable, overcome fear with courage, and make those thrills last. You can direct yourself to lower your defenses and open yourself to others. This is the essence of *90 Days of Love*.

In a nutshell, using these Five Secrets of Love as a guideline, this book will challenge you to master your thoughts and behaviors so as to experience connection, thereby releasing the tremendous love that dwells within.

Different Levels of Love

Love is an emotion that lets you know when you are experiencing connection. It goes without saying that you will experience connection differently and at different levels. Unfortunately, we use this one word "love" to describe all of them. Fortunately the Ancient Greeks used different words to express six different and distinct levels of connection.

Eros, or sexual desire, is connection on the physical level.

Ludus, or playful love, is a surface connection, not getting deep in any area.

Philia, or friendship, or brotherly love, is a connection on the mental and emotional levels.

Agape is universal love, or a giving of our self to others. It is love on the spiritual level and is expressed and felt through our contribution to humanity.

Pragma is love that survives and weathers over many obstacles and time. This is a connection on every level between two people, for it takes time to get through the many barriers we ourselves put in the path of love.

Philautia is self-love. As you love yourself, so will you love others. Or as Aristotle put it, "All friendly feelings for others are an extension of a person's feelings for their self."

These last four types of love, Philia, Agape, Pragma, and Philautia, are what the exercises in this book work to strengthen within you.

(Based on the Article 'The Ancient Greeks' 6 Words for Love (And Why Knowing Them Can Change Your Life)' [www.yesmagazine.org], and based on the book How Should We Live? Great Ideas From the Past for Everyday Life by Roman Krznaric)

A Little Bit About Feelings

Your feelings are wordless messages that your body "feels" when you are in the middle of an experience, whether real, perceived or imagined. Feelings are sourced from the nervous system and are part of the mind. Indeed, they are very powerful messages that pull the strings of your behaviors. For instance, you feel anger when you experience reality differently than you think it should be. From this anger you are compelled to yell, argue, get frustrated, withdraw, confront, complain, control or attempt to change other people's behavior. Another example is sadness. You feel sadness when you lose connection with a loved one. This leads you to cry, stay in bed, watch sad movies, listen to sad music, ignore texts and generally withdraw.

Your brain determines your emotional response, not an event that happens to you. Your feelings are triggered by either experiencing an event, perceiving that you experience an event, or by imagining that you experience an event. No event or person can make you feel anything. All of your feelings are determined by the neural pathways in your brain. You get angry because you already have the angry thought within you. The angry thought is only triggered. The same with love. To increase love, you must build or regrow those neural pathways for love.

The job of an emotional response is to compel a behavior. The emotion or feeling first starts with a thought, triggered from an event or your imagination. For instance, if you imagine losing the love of your life (the thought), then you will generate sadness (the feeling), which might make you cry, or check that the doors are locked, or call that person to see if they are safe (the behaviors).

Conversely, a behavior can trigger a feeling as well. For example, if you complain (the behavior), you will generate anger (the feeling). If you behave in a loving manner such as expressing empathy, care about someone's experience of life, become emotionally vulnerable, point out a person's greatness, support their dreams, then you will feel loving. You do not need to feel love to act loving. But you can act loving in order to feel love.

Thus, it's your thoughts and behaviors that shape your feelings.

If you imagine yourself as empathetic, caring, vulnerable, complimentary and supportive, you will feel love. In fact, anytime you feel in yourself what others are feeling, or see in yourself what others are experiencing, you will create empathy, which creates connection, which you experience as love.

The problem is that thoughts are programmed from childhood experiences to respond in a way that helped you survive childhood. What you imagine, perceive, or sense triggers childhood interpretations of events so that you will react in the same way that insured your survival. This explains why the world lacks love. Because once a child unwillingly learns to use powerful negative emotions to get what they want, they can never unlearn them until they put in the effort to reprogram their self.

The fact that thoughts trigger feelings is both good and bad. The good part is that you can generate any feeling you want by thinking about something that would normally trigger the feeling. If you want to feel love in your life, just think about love. You can either think love from your imagination or behave lovingly so as to change your thoughts to love.

The bad part is that if you are constantly producing negative feelings, you have to reprogram your thoughts. The exercises in *90 Days of Love* are designed to create new habits of loving thoughts and behaviors. But it's not easy—it's work. If reprogramming yourself was easy, you would have done it already. In fact, hardly anybody does it. So take this opportunity to create habitual thoughts and behaviors of love.

There is no right or wrong about feelings. The power comes in knowing you can work through the emotions to create the love and the life you want. How your thoughts drive your feelings, and how your feelings drive your behavior is of course according to your own brew of individuality.

True Love Is Inside the True You

Have you ever stopped to think that your ideas, thoughts, beliefs, prejudices, and rules about love may not be your own? We are master mimickers, and can easily incorporate other people's behaviors into our own. For instance, we may think that someone else is more successful than us, so unconsciously we imitate them in order to make ourselves successful. We learn about love (or lack of it) from our parents, family, friends, community, books, magazines, movies, songs, websites and especially from experiences with our lovers. We also express love based upon how we feel about ourselves.

Even though human individuals have many similarities, each of us are unique. Thus what works for one person may not work for another. We have to know what works for us individually. These exercises are designed for this exact discovery.

Here is the truth. You have everything inside of you that you need to be successful with love. This is because you are born with the neural wiring for love. Your brain is a social organ. When someone treats you in a way that you interpret as love, you respond positively. Moreover, humans are one of a handful of species that produce and react to the hormone oxytocin, better known as the cuddle hormone— the "molecule of monogamy." If love is difficult for you, it is because you have not had constant and continual experience with love. In other words, you are out of practice because you have not been stimulating those neural pathways that have been in place since you were born.

The bottom line is to trust yourself and learn what works for you. Have courage, take an emotional risk, be honest with yourself and others, and feel, maybe for the first time, what care and connection feel like.

In the long run, the benefits of being a loving person far outweigh the work and risks of building loving thoughts and behaviors. What's possible with love? A life-long intimate relationship, close friends, supporting family, rewarding career, meeting exciting people, becoming part of a community, inner calmness and peace, new positive experiences. Most of all, a brand new relationship with you, one built upon acceptance, trust and appreciation for yourself.

I can attest my own experience and growth to these exercises. I accept, trust and appreciate myself and know that my contribution to humanity matters. You, too, matter! Only you can contribute the uniqueness that is inside of you.

Love puts everyone on the same playing field. Love strengthens the weak and weakens the strong. Love connects all people. Love turns hope into knowing. Love returns brokenness to wholeness. Love turns lack into abundance. There is no upper limit to love.

How This Program Works

This program utilizes the Five Steps of Mastery.

Step 1: Intention.

This is the starting point. You have to intend to have more love in your life. Intention is very important because it is what keeps you committed to your goal, no matter what!

There are four parts to intention:

The Thought. For example, you think to yourself, *I want to be a loving person and to be loved. I am a loving person and am loved.*

Persistence. Continually thinking that thought, 24 hours a day, over many days, weeks, and months. In the case of this book, you must keep your intention in mind for at least 90 days.

Envision. See yourself being a loving person. Create a picture in your mind of yourself loving others and being loved by them. What does your life look like as a person who loves all people completely?

Feeling. What does being a loving person feel like? Imagine the feelings you will have as you perform acts of love, and your love life is running at 100%. Right at this moment, see and feel yourself in this way, because the future is created in the present.

Step 2: Knowledge.

You have to know how to create love. This book gives you many ideas and opportunities to do that.

Step 3: Practice.

These love exercises repeat through cycles that gradually get more difficult, just as a person would slowly learn piano, a sport, or anything else. With practice, it is safe to fail, and even expected. You might have to fail a few times before you succeed.

Step 4: Feedback.

Though taking in feedback can be difficult, you need to occasionally check in with your progress by receiving input from other people. Are you are coming across as loving or not? Feedback works best if you take it as being neutral, neither positive nor negative. See feedback as letting you know whether you are being effective or not. Although asking for feedback is scheduled in the 90 days, once a month ask the people who know you if they notice anything different. Remember, though, that all people look at you and the world through their own filters.

Step 5: Understanding.

Understanding is knowledge plus experience. Once you understand how to create a connection with a person, you will understand love, and better yet, you will understand how to create love with anybody.

Organization of the Program

90 Days of Love is organized into 7 categories that rotate through 13 weeks. It does not matter which day of the week you begin, though it may help to stay on track if you begin on a Sunday.

1st Day of Week: I AM

These exercises are personal reflections on loving yourself.

2nd Day of Week: BODY AND HEALTH

These exercises involve taking care of your body. You take care of things you love. So by loving your body, you will take care of it. Conversely, if you take care of your body, you love it.

You might sometimes think of yourself as mind, body and spirit. In truth, these are just parts of your wholeness, your mind-body-spirit. If you take care of one part, the other parts will improve as well.

3rd Day of Week: ABUNDANCE

These exercises are for switching your thinking toward abundance instead of scarcity—from thinking *There is not enough* to *There is enough and I can create more.* This directly relates to changing the thought of *I am not enough* to *I am enough.*

4th Day of Week: POSITIVE EMOTIONS AND EXPRESSIONS

Love can be expressed in many ways including gratitude, acceptance, forgiveness, honesty, vulnerability, or just catching up with a long lost friend. Either way, these are all forms of connection.

5th Day of Week: CONNECTION AND GIVING

Giving is a form of connection as well, as long as it is unconditional, from abundant thinking, and something that you possess that you can give to another human being. Experiencing love through giving is very rewarding.

6th Day of Week: INNER SELF AND VISION

These exercises are about pulling love out of your inner-self through your imagination, personal vision, and reflection. Seeing yourself as loving will slowly change you into a loving person.

7th Day of Week: LOVE FREELY

You are creative and imaginative, unique and different. So every seventh day is a space where you can do one of the exercises your way. Or if you need extra work in a certain area of your life, you can double up on an exercise here.

What You Will Need

• A quiet, undisturbed place to write for at least 10 minutes each day

• A large mirror. A bathroom mirror works. A full-length mirror is better.

• $20-200+. A few exercises suggest spending or giving away money. You have levels of giving and spending that make you uncomfortable. *90 Days of Love* is all about doing something different. As you push your boundaries with love, this is also an opportunity to push your boundaries with giving.

• A daily reminder. Life happens. Make sure you have a method to redirect you back to these exercises. This program works! Do whatever it takes to come back and <u>stay on track</u>.

• An extra journal (optional). Space and lines for journaling have been included in this book. It might be good to have a extra writing paper available.

A Note on Journaling

A journal is a daily writing that chronicles your journey. The word "journal" comes from the Latin *diurnalis* which means "of the day" or "daily." The purpose of journaling is to reinforce your experience during the exercise. It is important to pay attention to your thoughts, feelings and behaviors. Then you can write them down while at the same time allowing yourself to examine them in detail.

If journaling is not your usual thing, here are some suggested questions to reflect upon.

• Was this exercise easy or difficult?

• Did I notice anything new about myself?

• What thoughts came up for me?

• Were my thoughts different from what I always imagined about myself or other people?

• What have I learned about love so far?

If you are having negative thoughts, emotions or reactions, write about them in the 3rd person. Instead of writing, "I felt angry about that exercise!" write instead, "He/She/(your name) felt angry about that exercise!" This will create distance between your conscious and your more primitive brain. With this distance you can reflect upon the source of these negative thoughts while at the same time giving yourself a space to create new, loving thoughts.

The Purpose

The purpose of this book is not to put the secret of love into words, but to draw it out of you and put it in your own hands, as a paintbrush to a painter who wishes to create his or her life on canvas.

Now it is your turn to draw out your own love and paint your own picture called *My Life*. In fact, your painting is not a still life, but it is a movie full of action, adventure, romance, and even cliffhangers. Maybe at times, you will see yourself as Aladdin where you rub the lamp of your imagination and make a wish from the genie of your own power. Make a wish for every person, including you, to step into their own amazing adventure of love.

Because of my own struggles with love and relationships, I know your heartaches, pains, betrayals, and losses of love. I have felt the same sadness, anger, and fear. I understand the anxiety, insecurity, need to control and need to withdraw. I have experienced all of these. And it is through these many obstacles that I found a pathway toward activating my love center. *90 Days of Love* is a smoother and more direct passage to the higher ground called love. May these exercises lead you to an amazing love life.

What to do when you hit
THE WALL

There is a good chance that at least one of these exercises will be extremely challenging for you, so much so that you will be tempted to abandon the exercise or discontinue the program. For some people, the first exercise, as simple as it is, brought up a tremendous amount of negative self-thinking that tested the activation of their love center. If or when this happens to you, I urge you to continue.

It's also OK to repeat an exercise for several days, or take a break, or go in a different order, or skip around. There is no prize for doing all 90 exercises in 90 days. But here *is* a reward for exercising and strengthening your love center; your fulfilling life. Know that on the other side of every challenging exercise is the love you've been hoping for in your life.

Your body and mind are designed to keep you safe. Thus when you venture beyond your comfort zone, negative feelings arise that compel you to fall back into the behaviors that keep you safe. Know that behind those behaviors are just thoughts and feelings. Yes, they are real and a part of your wholeness, but they are not permanent and will go away if you continue with *90 Days of Love*. True Love is being vulnerable AND strong. True Love is being both accepting of where you are AND knowing everything can get better. True Love is seeing the uniqueness of all (non-judgmental) AND seeing everyone as part of a single wholeness (connection).

Getting to True Love takes practice to push beyond your comfort zones into areas where you feel unsafe and uncomfortable. When you feel those negative feelings that are bullying you to pull back, that is when you push forward. Keep going! Keep climbing! The love you want is on the other side.

REMEMBER:

Think love, act loving, and soon you will be loving.

Enjoy your journey through *90 Days of Love*. More importantly, I can't wait to see the new, loving you on day 91!

The Exercises

Week 1 - Days 1-7

First Day of the Week:

I AM

Love Exercise Day 1

Look in the mirror for 5 minutes without saying anything.

Journal for 10 minutes.

(Was the experience easy or difficult?
Notice anything new or different?)

Today is about taking a closer look at yourself. What are your thoughts? What are you telling yourself about love?

Love Secret #3 states that "You are able to consciously create love." Love Secret #4 states that "Your thoughts and behaviors affect your love." This means that what you think about love, what you are telling yourself, is affecting the amount of love you have in your life. The good news is that, because of this, you have control of your love life. The bad news is that you have to choose to create love. This means that if you want more love in your life, take responsibility for your thoughts about love and yourself. But the first step is to recognize and acknowledge what you are telling yourself.

Enjoy the rest of your day!

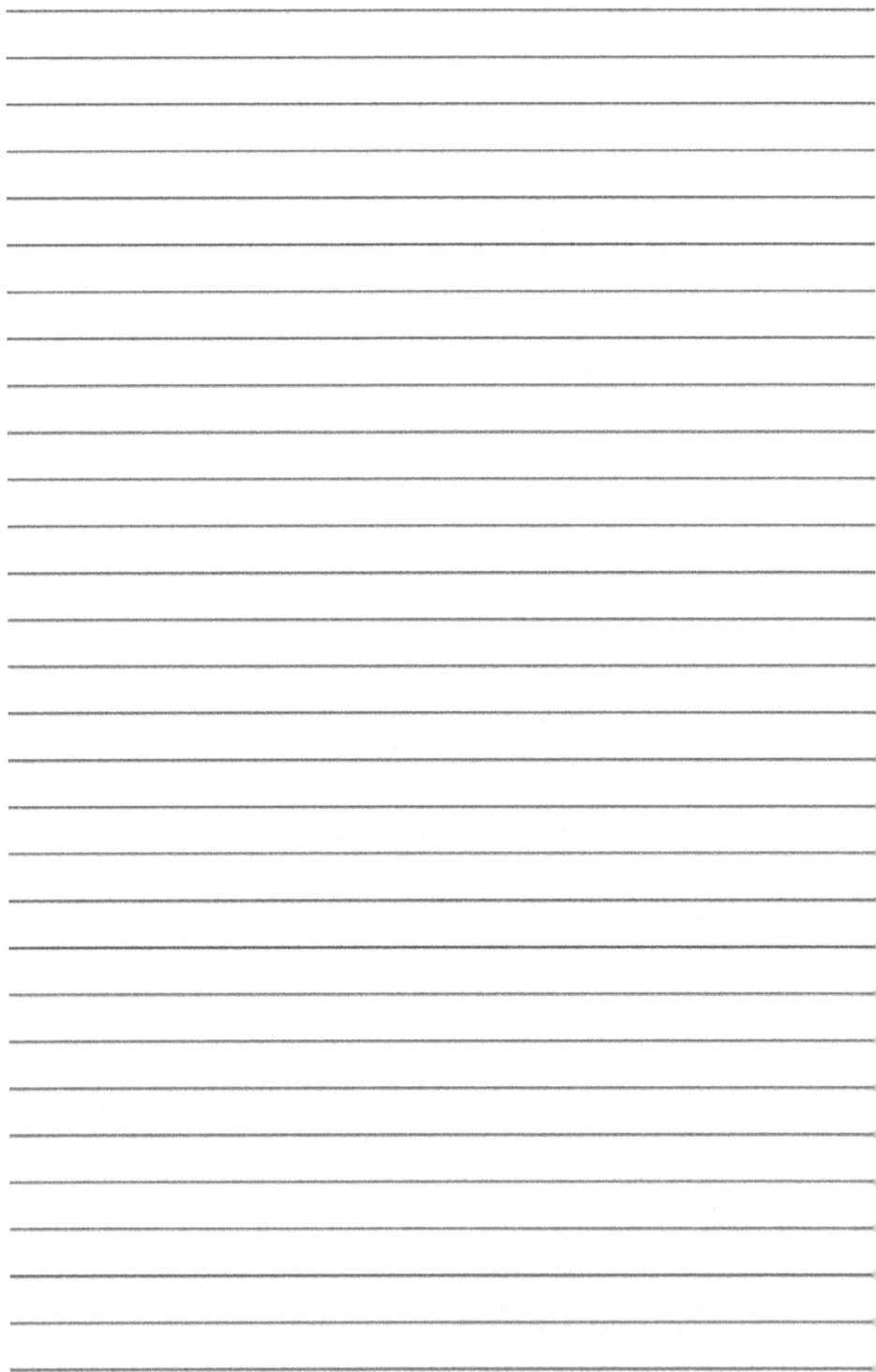

Second Day of the Week:

BODY AND HEALTH

Love Exercise Day 2

Eat healthy all day today.

Journal in the evening.

(How did you feel today? If you didn't eat healthy, was there a reason? How did you respond to eating or not eating healthy?)

You are an integration of body, mind, and spirit, put together into one person called I! If you take care of one part of yourself, the other parts will be lifted up as well. Today is all about taking care of your precious body. Eating healthy is love for the body. In truth, you will take care of your body—not because you dislike it—but because you love it!

Healthy can be fun!

Third Day of the Week:

ABUNDANCE

Love Exercise Day 3

Look around your environment and with everything you see, say, "I love (___)." For instance, "I love (that chair). I love (this picture)." Whatever you see, say to yourself that you love it.

Journal for 10 minutes.

(Was the experience easy or difficult? Notice anything new or different?)

You are a part of your environment and your environment is a part of you. When you are in a relationship in which you uphold your "part," then you are in Partnership.

This exercise is about being in partnership with yourself. Partnership is a specific kind of relationship that you have with someone, including yourself, where you agree to work together to create something. In a sense, with this exercise, you are agreeing with yourself to love all things around you. The result is an abundance of love.

Though this exercise may seem simple, silly or odd, it is effective. Turning on your love center "switch" is as easy as saying "I love . . . "

Fourth Day of the Week:

POSITIVE EMOTIONS AND EXPRESSIONS

Love Exercise Day 4

Have a No Argument Day.

At the end of the day, journal for at least 10 minutes.

This exercise is about taking control of your emotions. Emotions can be considered as primitive thoughts. They are triggered from the powerhouse of your mind—the subconscious. Emotions are so powerful that they compel you to behave one way even while your conscious mind is thinking that you want to behave another way. We've all had this experience! For instance, you say you will not eat another potato chip, then you do. Or you say you don't want to fight, but get so angry, you can't help it.

Be conscious today of your emotions that compel you to argue, whether you voice those arguments or not. Be mindful that emotions come from beliefs that have lodged themselves into your powerful subconscious. These beliefs rear their ugly heads in order to compel others to conform to you through your anger (the emotion) and arguments (the behavior). In other words, you get angry and argue because there is a difference between what you believe should happen, and reality. As you argue, others will begin to get in alignment with your beliefs. In a sense, anger is a power that causes reality to abide to your beliefs. Simply put, your anger gets others to change real quick! Though only temporarily. This is the opposite of love.

By having a No Argument Day, you are giving love a chance to take root inside of you.

So have fun on this No Argument Day, even if you have to bite your tongue.

🌉 Fifth Day of the Week:

CONNECTION AND GIVING

Love Exercise Day 5

Do a small, nice thing anonymously for someone without
any expectation of anything in return.

Afterwards, journal.

There is a universal law that states "What you put out comes back to you." Another way of expressing this is Givers Gain. In fact, the more you freely give unconditionally, the more you will gain. And this works for love as much as for anything else.

Unconditional giving in itself is the hallmark of love. Unconditional means that there are no strings attached to the gift. The receiver gets to do whatever they want with the gift including giving it away, throwing it away, or even just forgetting about it. In order for the gift to be completely unconditional, you must allow the recipient to have this freedom. If empowering others with choice is your challenge today, it's possible this lesson about giving is a gift to you.

So put out a little love today. I promise it will come back to you, though most likely not from the person to whom you gave. The universe likes to have its fun, too!

Be creative with this exercise!

OO Sixth Day of the Week:

INNER SELF AND VISION

Love Exercise Day 6

Find a quiet place to sit undisturbed. Relax. For 10 minutes, reflect on how you felt before and after each exercise this week. See love growing inside of you.

Journal.

For a small amount of time today, become familiar with the thoughts in your mind. Do you have an inner negative chatterbox? What percentage of your thoughts leaves you feeling good?

Your inner world projects onto the outer world. You can only see the outer world from your own perception, which creates your perspective. Ask yourself if the negativity of the outside world is a reflection of an inner negative thought pattern. Perhaps your reality reflects an inner broken heart — disappointments, insecurities, some terrible event?

Becoming aware of your thoughts and feelings and how they cause you to see and react to your environment is the first step toward growing love. The second step is to put aside negative thoughts and beliefs in order to allow your mind to see the world "as is." This is known as acceptance.

Choose to see the world as it is and you will have taken a great step toward love. If this is initially difficult or you, keep working on it. It can take time to remove the judgments you have put on the world. This is why it is so important to see love growing on the inside, because you will also see love growing on the outside.

Have an amazing day of discovery!

♥ ## Seventh Day of the Week:

LOVE FREELY

Love Exercise Day 7

Pick one of the exercises from the past week to do over again. Add your own personal touch, variation or flavor, if you wish. Or invent your own love exercise to do today and share it with our community.

Remember to journal!

Here is a recap of The Five Secrets of Love:

#1: You are capable of realizing your dreams of love.

#2: Love is the emotion of connection.

#3: You are able to consciously create love.

#4: Your thoughts and behaviors affect your love.

#5: The more you connect with people, the more they will connect with you.

I hope that you are beginning to see that you are in the driver's seat of your loving life. Love is and has been always inside of you. Through these exercises, you are activating and reinforcing the love center in your brain. No matter how you have done these exercises, your love will have grown.

Are you beginning to see that there is more than one way to love? The more different people you connect with, the more different ways of loving you will experience. Some will be easy to love. Some very challenging. But just like anything in life, if you conquer the challenging obstacles, all the other obstacles become easier. So today, give yourself a challenging love exercise and remember that success and failure are just feedback.

With all the love in my heart, I salute you for making it through the first week!

Week 2 - Days 8-14

First Day of the Week:

I AM

Love Exercise Day 8

Look in the mirror for 5 minutes repeating to yourself, "I am love."

Journal for 10 minutes.

Recall that Love Secret #2 states that "Love is the emotion of connection." By telling yourself that you are love, you are reminding yourself that you have the amazing capability to connect with other people on any level. More importantly, you will be able to connect easily with your inner greatness, reminding yourself of all you have to contribute to this world.

You are capable of realizing your dreams of love (Love Secret #1).

Enjoy the rest of your day!

_____

_____

_____

_____

_____

Second Day of the Week:

BODY AND HEALTH

Love Exercise Day 9

Treat yourself to your favorite healthy, whole food.

Journal.

Celebrate you today! And know that your body will thoroughly delight in getting its favorite food. Optimal health comes from balance. So make sure you balance out healthy foods with natural treats (one natural treat equals a large amount of healthy food). If your favorite food is healthy, celebrate the fact that every meal for you is an adventure in hardy balance. And if you get a smile in the bargain, then it is well worth it!

Hooray!

Third Day of the Week:

ABUNDANCE

Love Exercise Day 10

Take all of the cash and coins out of your purse or wallet and put it in a pile in front of you. Tell yourself, "I love what I can do with this money. I can do _____ or I can buy _____."

In your journal, write down everything that comes to mind.

This exercise is about checking in with your relationship with money.

Do you think in terms of abundance or scarcity? Of what you have or what you do not have? What you are capable of or what you are not capable of?

Abundance is distinctly different from wealth. Wealth is the accumulation of things. Abundance is the ability to create what you want, whenever you want. If you are able to create what you want, you will never run out of it because you can just make more. This goes for love as well as money.

Think of what you have created so far and rejoice in your ability to create. All people have this ability, though only a few use it. Because of this, creating abundance can seem like a superpower when in truth, it is a natural human ability.

You are a creation machine!

_____

_____

_____

_____

_____

_____

_____

_____

_____

_____

_____

_____

_____

_____

_____

_____

_____

_____

_____

_____

_____

Fourth Day of the Week:

POSITIVE EMOTIONS AND EXPRESSIONS

Love Exercise Day 11

Create an Acceptance List.
Write a list of all the things that bother you about
yourself. At the bottom write, "I am grateful for all of
this for it has made me who I am today."

Journaling about this can be very powerful.

A key component of love is acceptance. Even more than that, when you are in acceptance, you see things as they are in the moment. Because of this, love always brings you into the moment. In fact, love is the moment.

When you connect with other people, it is because you are being present with them. At the moment of connection, you are seeing "what is" as opposed to "what you think it is." This is acceptance. This is love.

By creating an acceptance list, you are acknowledging your whole self that exists in this present moment. By being grateful, you are accepting that every previous moment happened for a purpose.

If you find yourself resisting being grateful for those parts of yourself that you do not like, today is the day to break through that resistance and create positive feelings for yourself. Keep going!

People cannot love that which you do not reveal to them. Most likely those parts of yourself that you want to hide need love, first from yourself, then from others. By being grateful for all of yourself, and accepting your wholeness, you give permission for others to love every aspect of you.

You are here for a purpose! You will need your whole self to fulfill it.

_____

_____

_____

_____

_____

_____

_____

_____

_____

_____

_____

_____

_____

_____

_____

_____

Fifth Day of the Week:

CONNECTION AND GIVING

Love Exercise Day 12

Ask someone, "How can I help you today?" Extra points for asking, "How can I love you today?" Whatever their answer, if it's something you can give, give it. If not, find out where or from whom they can get help.

Afterwards, journal.

Last week I talked about the universal law that states "What you put out comes back to you." Today's exercise is about ramping up the action on this universal law.

Sometimes, because of beliefs, expectations or assumptions, you think people need something when in fact they do not. When you want to help someone, ask them if they actually want help. You might assume that what you are offering will be beneficial, when in fact, to the person who is receiving your thoughtful gift, it is not. This is one of those lovely human faults.

Today is about helping people by doing exactly what it is they are asking. The same goes for love. Many times we love people in ways that they do not recognize or acknowledge as love.

To love someone, you have to know how they experience love. Once, someone bought me a pair of shoes. At the time, I didn't think much about it because to me, receiving gifts didn't trigger my love center. Thus the gift giver didn't get the loving reaction they thought I would have. Years later, I realized that this was an act of love. This awkward situation could have easily been remedied by the question, "How can I love you today?" Asking this question is essential in turning a relationship into a love partnership.

You can do it!

⬭⬤⬭ Sixth Day of the Week:

INNER SELF AND VISION

Love Exercise Day 13

Find a quiet place to sit undisturbed. Relax. Breathe (6 seconds in, 6 seconds out.) For 10 minutes, think of all the people you have loved in your life. Reflect on how it feels to love these people. See love growing inside of you.

Journal.

In your life, you have already loved greatly. And since love is the emotion of connection (Love Secret #2), you already have connected with people. Even if those loved ones are no longer with you, or they are no longer connected to you, today is about celebrating and being grateful for having had those connections. Take ten minutes reminiscing the awesome feeling of being connected to another human being.

Also take a few minutes to see yourself creating new connections. This is love growing inside of you. Do not pick and choose who you imagine connecting with, for you are capable of loving any and every person.

Have a beautiful day!

♥ Seventh Day of the Week:

LOVE FREELY

Love Exercise Day 14

Pick one of the exercises from the past week to do over again. Add your own personal touch, variation or flavor if you wish. Or invent your own love exercise to do today and share it with our community.

Remember to journal!

Keep putting your fantastic, imaginative, fun-loving self into practicing love today. As you may recall, the third and fourth steps in becoming a master are practice and feedback.

What is your own internal feedback? Do you notice anything different about you? Are you feeling more loving? Are you more patient with people? More interested, accepting, communicative? If so, keep going. Imagine what eleven more weeks will get you! If not, then know that often times when you are working on rebuilding skills (and connecting with people is a skill), your brain can bring up bad feelings. Keep spending the 10-20 minutes a day working on attracting more love into your life. At some point, your brain will begin to reward you with good feelings and better relationships.

Congratulations on completing your second week!

Read the About Love section of the book, if you haven't read it yet.

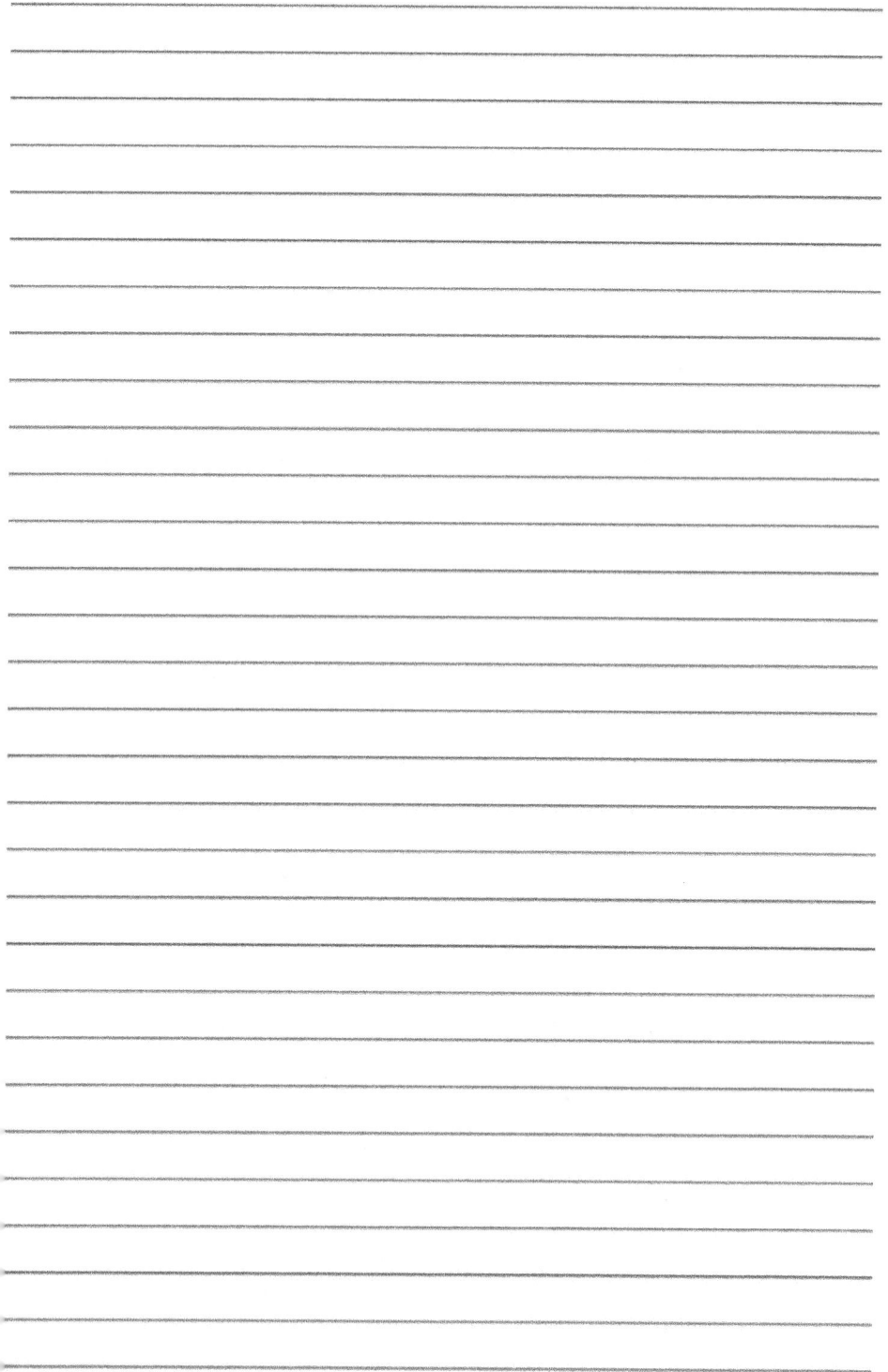

Week 3 - Days 15-21

👁 First Day of the Week:

I AM

Love Exercise Day 15

Look in the mirror for 5 minutes repeating,
"I love my flaws. I love my imperfections. I love my
mistakes. I love my weaknesses. I love my pains. I love
my fears."

Journal for 10 minutes.

This may be one of the most difficult exercises, especially if your self-image, the image you have of yourself in your mind, is different than the image you see in the mirror. This exercise is about getting your self-image and your actual image to be in alignment. You begin to do this by looking at those actual parts of yourself that you don't like and accepting them.

Hold in your heart that love means acceptance. You cannot connect with yourself until you see yourself as you are, just as you cannot connect with another person unless you see them as they are.

Acceptance does not mean that you don't want things to be different about yourself, or that you are resigning yourself to be the same for the rest of your life. Of course you want to have new experiences. That is why you are doing these exercises!

The point is to realize that every human has flaws, imperfections, mistakes, weaknesses, pains and fears. To love is to see these in a person and still do everything you can to connect with them.

I am amazed by your courage to come this far!

_____

_____

_____

_____

_____

_____

_____

_____

_____

_____

_____

_____

_____

_____

_____

_____

_____

_____

Second Day of the Week:

BODY AND HEALTH

Love Exercise Day 16

Get a facial, massage, manicure, haircut or shave;
or anything that involves healing touch.
Have fun taking care of yourself! Whoopee!

Journal.

You deserve self-love. The more you take care of yourself, the more you will love you.

If none of these work for you, you could trade back massages with a loved one. Or take a hot bath with scented bath salts. Whatever it is, go crazy! It's the loving you that you want to reward. For whatever you give attention to will grow.

I love this exercise!

Third Day of the Week:

ABUNDANCE

Love Exercise Day 17

Find something of yours that you can easily replace. Give it to someone whether there is a reason or not.

Journal.

The great paradox of life is that the truly valuable things are given to you for free. Life, loved ones, friends, imagination, memory, intelligence, your senses, smiles, laughter, etc. The list goes on and on. On the other hand, many of the things you think are valuable are all replaceable. Sometimes you will find it harder to give away something you paid for rather than something that was given to you for free.

Pick something good!

Fourth Day of the Week:

POSITIVE EMOTIONS AND EXPRESSIONS

Love Exercise Day 18

Make a Forgiveness List of all the people whom you feel have hurt you.
Going down the list, think about forgiving each person.
Then make a Forgiveness List for all of the times you may have hurt others, no matter how slight.
Going down the list, think about asking that person for forgiveness.
Then forgive yourself.

Journal optional.

Forgiveness literally takes a few seconds. If you are holding onto hurts, now is the time to let them go through forgiveness. Start the process. I promise, it will hurt much less than the original event (if at all.)

Once you realize that forgiveness is just a thought that you choose to have, you can practice Instant Forgiveness! Imagine forgiving anyone who hurts you the instant it happens. Then you can immediately get on with your amazing life.

67

I hope you see the possibilities for your life that being loving attracts to you.

Fifth Day of the Week:

CONNECTION AND GIVING

Love Exercise Day 19

Volunteer for something today.
Or do an act of charity that you would normally regard as
meaningless.

Afterwards, journal.

If you normally do not volunteer for good causes, today is about doing something different with your time. Watch out, you might enjoy it!

Or if you often volunteer, do an act of charity that you normally believe would not have a positive impact.

Today is about giving your time and talent to other people. Volunteering, or being charitable, is an opportunity to experience the fact that no person is any more human than any other person, regardless of status or wealth.

Every person is capable of love, so practice connecting with other people. Ask them for their stories and other open-ended questions. See where people are stuck. Give compassion and overwhelming love, for this is how you open the doors of opportunity for others to walk through.

69

Have fun today!

⊙⊙ Sixth Day of the Week:

INNER SELF AND VISION

Love Exercise Day 20

Find a quiet place to sit undisturbed. Relax. Breathe (6 seconds in, 6 seconds out.) For 10-20 minutes, watch the movement of the moon, shadows, sun or clouds by comparing their positions to a fixed object. Reflect on how everything is in motion and changing.

Journal.

Today is about appreciating the moment and how it flows through time. Every moment is an opportunity to love. And every time you love, you grow.

Everything is changing at every moment, including yourself and other people, though the changes may be gradual and unnoticeable. There are only two ways of changing, either growing or decaying. Stability is an illusion. If you are not growing in love, your love is decaying.

90 Days of Love is just to get you started. Think of how you are after twenty days of growing love. Think about 100 days from now. 1000 days. 5000 days. Every day of love is another step in an amazing journey.

"The most important step a person can take. It's not the first one, is it? It's the next one. Always the next step."
- Brandon Sanderson, *Oathbringer*.

Enjoy this amazing step!

Seventh Day of the Week:

LOVE FREELY

Love Exercise Day 21

Pick one of the exercises from the past week to do over again. Add your own personal touch, variation or flavor if you wish. Or invent your own love exercise to do today and share it with our community.

Remember to journal!

Put your brilliant, amazing, creative self into practicing love. To master anything, you have to practice and get feedback. As you practice, be aware of feedback from people. Does your family, friends or co-workers notice anything different about you? Are you acting more loving, speaking more caring, looking more radiant? Any amount of positive feedback, whether people express it or not, is telling you that you are increasing activity in your love center. The more you practice, the more positive feedback you will get. Keep going and keep learning, no matter how you feel.

If you haven't received feedback, don't worry. You will as long as you continue doing these exercises.

Congratulations on completing three weeks!

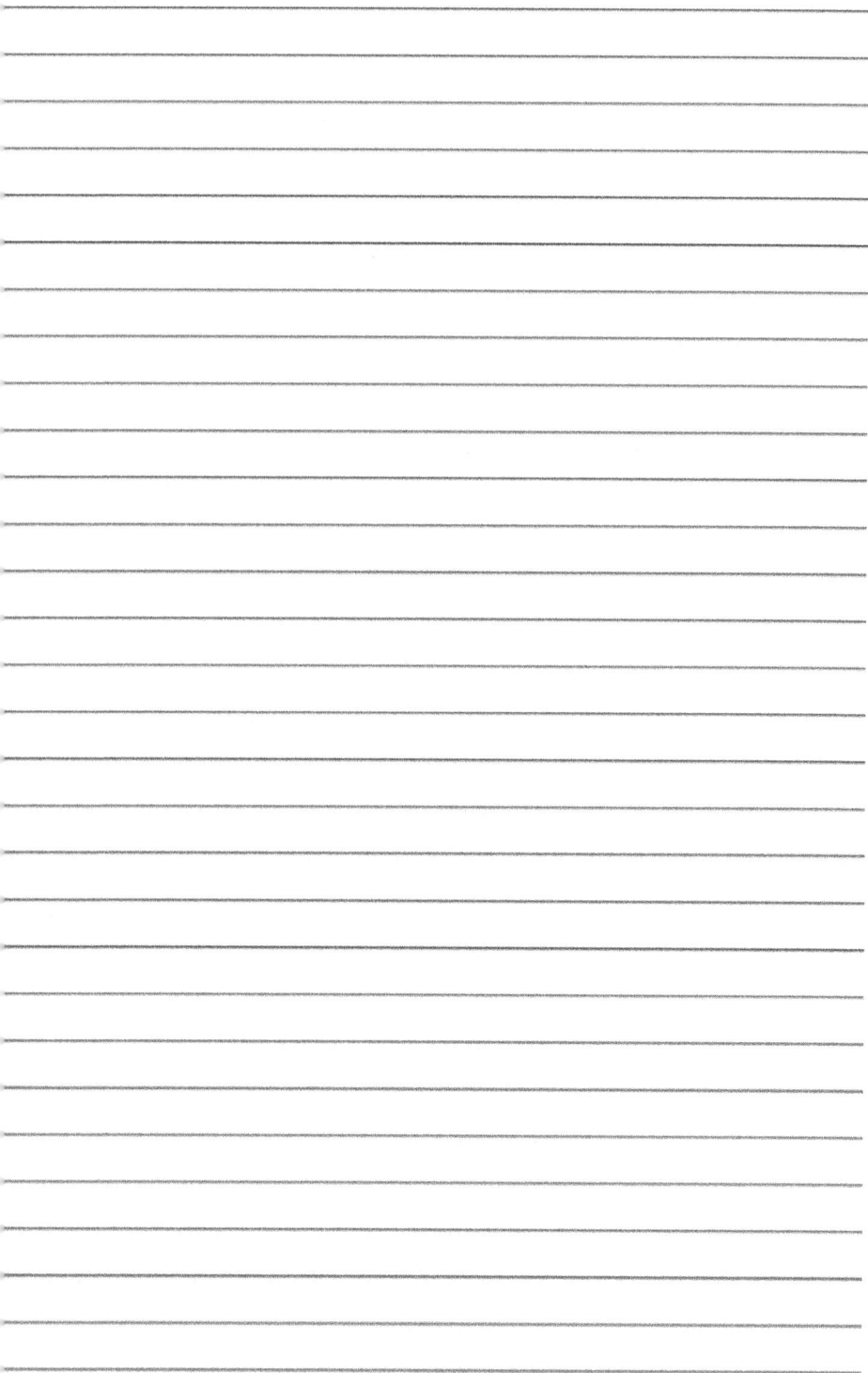

Week 4 - Days 22-28

First Day of the Week:

I AM

Love Exercise Day 22

Look in the mirror for 5 minutes telling yourself,
"I accept you just as you are."

Journal.

LOVE REVEALS THE PRESENT MOMENT

Loving yourself does not mean you are forever stuck as you are in the present moment. Loving yourself tells you where you are now so that you can create an accurate path to where you want to go.

The truth is that if you do not love yourself as you are now, you will probably not love yourself as you are later.

I know that sometimes loving is not easy. I admire your bravery as much as I admire you!

Second Day of the Week:

BODY AND HEALTH

Love Exercise Day 23

Give your body a gift. Some examples: new shoes, socks, jewelry, clothes, hat, accessory, watch, or scarf. Scented candles, incense, perfume. A small treat like gourmet chocolate or small dessert. Tell yourself that you deserve it.

Journal.

There is a difference between earning something and deserving something. "Earning" is more about receiving something in exchange for doing something. "Deserving" is more about receiving something as a benefit of the quality of your beingness.

For example, pretend your significant other goes away for a business trip. They do their work and then return home, earning money for the work completed. For a reward, you suggest that they deserve a day off. Unfortunately your significant other did a lousy job on the trip, causing delays and extra work. At this point, though your significant other earned the money, they may not feel like they deserve a day off.

The point of today's exercise and this story is this: when you connect with others and feel love for them, you feel deserving of love. If you feel that you do not deserve to give yourself anything today, ask yourself, "When will I feel deserving of love?" Are you being loving? Are your expectations too high? How about this: just accept that whatever love you give to yourself, more love will come back to you in return.

Think of Givers Gain. As you receive love, you will have love to give. Thus you will gain more love, and have more to give, and so on, up and up.

That's what we call a love spiral!

If you feel like you are struggling to move up this spiral, seek support. Take a friend with you and share with them your intentions and struggles with love.

Third Day of the Week:

ABUNDANCE

Love Exercise Day 24

Have a Yes! day. Say "Yes!" to things you always wanted to say "Yes!" to, but haven't. Also, say "Yes!" to people to which you always wanted to say "Yes!" to, but haven't.

Journal.

Warren Buffett has stated that the number one word successful people use is "No." This is a powerful word for staying focused on goals and setting boundaries, which you need for growing, staying healthy and remaining balanced.

But today is about being open to imagined possibilities in which you for some reason have shut the door. And this requires a "Yes!" Anytime you want to create an abundance of something, it will require a "Yes!"

I use an exclamation point on the "Yes!" because emotion is needed behind every affirmation. Your emotions are the powerhouse of your life. Though your conscious thinking directs your life, the energy needed to propel you forward comes from your emotions. So whatever you do today, immerse yourself in the positive feeling of the action. Because at some point, Warren Buffet also has to say "Yes!"

I am so excited that something new is waiting for you today!

Fourth Day of the Week:

POSITIVE EMOTIONS AND EXPRESSIONS

Love Exercise Day 25

Reconnect with one person from your past with which you had a connection.

Journal.

Connection takes no time at all, especially with someone special in your past, whether they are family, friend, colleague, schoolmate or lover. When you reconnect with someone, it is like being transported back in time to the last moment you did connect. Suddenly the past seems to catch up with the present as you update the relationship into the NOW. This is because connection is not a function of time. When you experience connection, you are brought into the moment. Suddenly age, distance, physical appearance, circumstances, or life events do not matter. What matters is being present in the moment with another human being.

Say "Hi" from me!

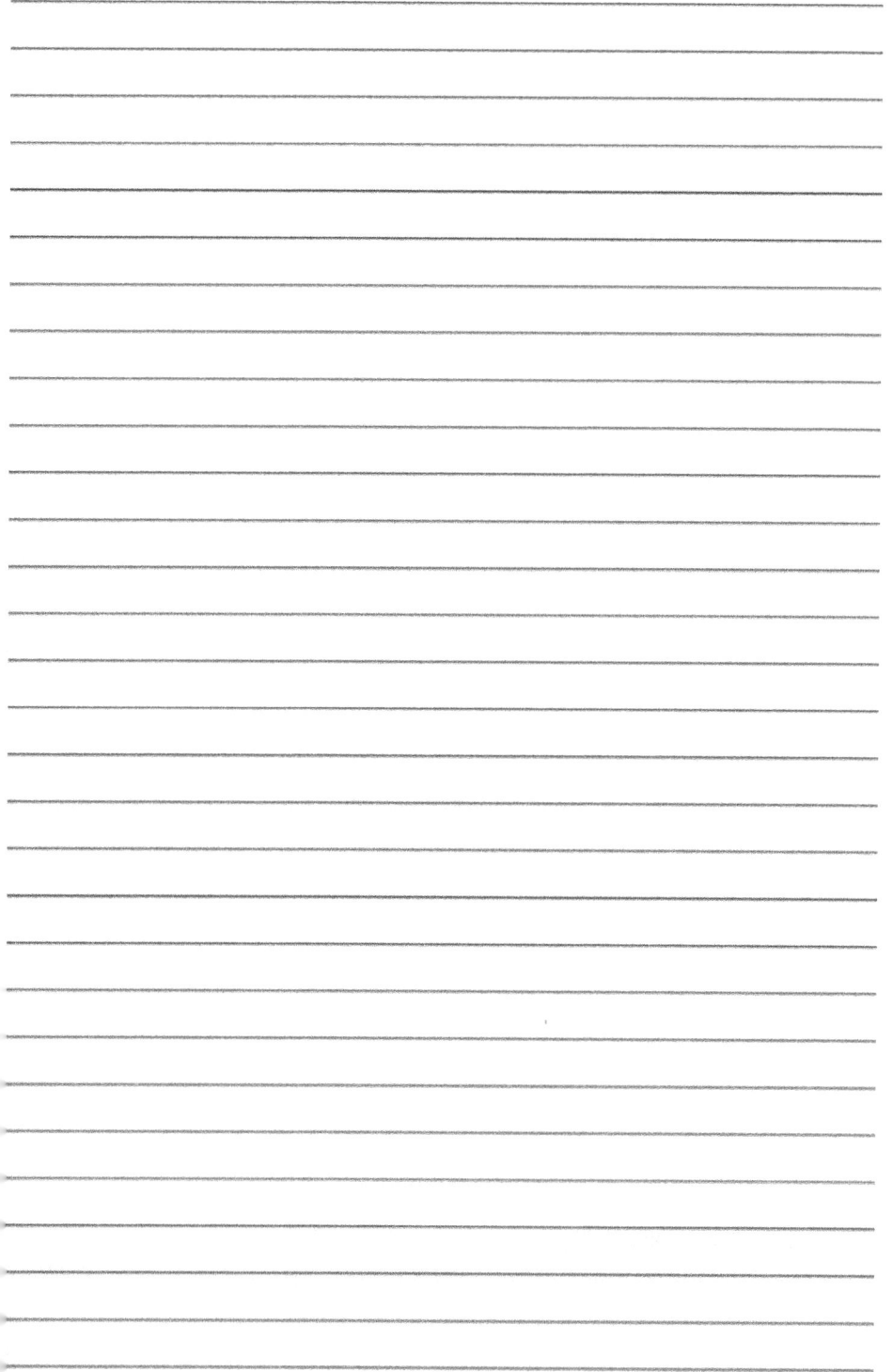

Fifth Day of the Week:

CONNECTION AND GIVING

Love Exercise Day 26

Write down on a piece of paper something of your time, talent, or money that you can give, along with your name and phone number. Give it to a friend with the instructions for them to give it away.

Journal.

When you give, you never know when, where, or from whom you will receive the gift back. So in a sense, it does not matter the person you give to. All that matters is giving. And it doesn't take much. Most experts in giving recommend that for every dollar you earn, you give ten cents away, or 10%. That's it! Like I said above, it can be given to anyone, as long as it is unconditional.

Though this exercise does not necessarily connect yourself with other people, it does connect you with a much bigger entity, the universe itself. Since the universe gives to you unconditionally, the simple act of giving unconditionally puts you in alignment with all creation. Besides, your true treasures to give are always free and abundant. Also, when you give a part of yourself, you make room for something more valuable to come into your life!

The smallest things make the biggest difference!

⊶ Sixth Day of the Week:

INNER SELF AND VISION

Love Exercise Day 27

Find a quiet place to sit undisturbed. Relax. Breathe (6 seconds in, 6 seconds out.) For 10 minutes, think of all the people you will see, meet, and interact with today. See yourself loving them unconditionally. See love growing inside of you.

Journal.

Today is about allowing your conscious to learn from your imagination and take that lesson of love into reality.

In order to consciously create anything, you have to see it first in your imagination. This is true for love and connection as it is for anything else. Your imagination is the playground in which you get to act out different scenarios until you come upon the one that creates the most love.

For example, have you been on a date that didn't go very well? In your imagination, you get to redo that date until you change the outcome to something you would have wanted. Then you can apply it to a future date.

See love growing inside of you. You can represent love as a growing plant, tree, light, shining star, or whatever works for you. Keep this image with you.

What an amazing day you are going to have!

_____
_____
_____
_____
_____
_____
_____
_____
_____
_____
_____
_____
_____
_____
_____
_____
_____
_____
_____
_____
_____
_____

♥ Seventh Day of the Week:

LOVE FREELY

Love Exercise Day 28

Pick one of the exercises from the past week to do over again. Add your own personal touch, variation or flavor if you wish. Or invent your own love exercise to do today and share it with our community.

Read back over your journal to see all that you have created. Reflect on where you are now compared to where you were.

Continue to journal on your personal discoveries!

How do you want to be loved? The answer to this question depends on your needs and wants. Yet, no matter your needs and wants, you have to employ honest communication to express them to your partner. That at least puts you and your romantic other on the road to Partnership.

To create a loving and lasting Partnership, there are four Pillars of Partnership that you must build upon.

1. Self-love (What this book is all about)

2. A Method of Honest Communication

3. Balance

4. Release Control (The 2nd Law of Love)

You can learn more about romantic Partnerships at www.partnershipandlove.com. Congratulations on finishing your fourth week! You are well on your way to mastering love.

_____
_____
_____
_____
_____
_____
_____
_____
_____
_____
_____
_____
_____
_____
_____
_____

Week 5 - Days 29-35

First Day of the Week:

I AM

Love Exercise Day 29

Looking in the mirror for 5 minutes, tell yourself that you love everything which you have never loved about yourself, including everything in the past that you view as negative.

Journal.

This exercise may be another difficult one. But look at it this way. If you are able to love anything that happened to you in the past, you will be able to love anything that happens in the future. Also, if you love all that you are now, you will love all that you will become. In short, how you love yourself today will be how you love yourself tomorrow.

If you put water in a cup with holes, it will never fill up. The same goes for people and love. Your negative thinking and negative feelings are holes. When you create love, it will just run out of these holes and you will never feel full of love. This will leave you unfulfilled, resentful, and make it difficult to maintain a relationship. So today, do the serious work and make sure all of your holes are patched up with love. Connect with yourself today. You are the authority of your life.

There is no love pill. To create self-love, you have to do the work. And if need be, get support! You have come this far. Keep going.

If you can conquer this difficult obstacle, all the others will become easier!

Second Day of the Week:

BODY AND HEALTH

Love Exercise Day 30

*Do something for your body that you normally never do.
For example, take a martial arts lesson, hire a trainer,
follow an exercise video on Youtube, take a dance lesson, go
for a walk, jog or run.*

Journal.

Taking care of yourself sometimes requires doing things before you want to do them. For instance, you may not feel like getting a martial arts lesson, but you go ahead and do it anyways. Or you may not feel like going for a walk, but you still go outside and start walking. When you begin to do something, regardless of how you feel, typically you only begin to feel like doing it after you start doing it. Getting past that starting point often means taking charge of yourself regardless of your inner talk.

After you do today's exercise, consider this; love often requires starting to love before you feel like loving. Sometimes you have to start with the behavior and then the feeling will follow. This is where your conscious ability to drive yourself stands out. You are in charge of your behaviors. You are in charge of your love center!

Making a decision and then taking action on it is the essence of integrity. To maintain integrity, there may be times you have to do something regardless of how you are feeling at that moment. This is why having the ability to call forth love to help you take action can make a powerful, positive impact in your life and relationships.

This is why I am encouraging you to choose love and live in integrity. Partnership is the process of using love and integrity to create the relationship you want.

Being in Partnership with someone is the same as being in Partnership with yourself. You make an agreement to do something that you want, and then you do it. Like I said before, all of the qualities that create success are already inside of you, including love and integrity. It's just a matter of strengthening them and letting them guide the way.

I'm rooting for you!

Third Day of the Week:

ABUNDANCE

Love Exercise Day 31

You have an abundance of good things to give. Give a heartfelt compliment, hug, smile, or affirmation to everyone you see today.

Journal.

If you recall from Day 10, abundance is the ability to create what you want, whenever you want. This is different from wealth, which is the result of accumulation. Certainly, though, one can create wealth from abundance.

Since compliments, hugs, smiles and affirmations can be created whenever you want, you have them in abundance. This means that no matter how many you give away, you will always have more to give.

What else do you have in abundance?

_____

_____

_____

_____

_____

_____

_____

Fourth Day of the Week:

POSITIVE EMOTIONS AND EXPRESSIONS

Love Exercise Day 32

Apologize to someone who deserves your apology.

Journal.

Building bridges is a metaphor used for creating connections with people. Likewise, burning bridges is used to represent disconnecting with people. Expressing remorse is about re-building a bridge where one once stood. True love does not care about intentions. People can get hurt through your words or actions even though injury was the farthest thing from your mind. By offering an apology, connection can be re-established. Know that connection is the true goal, not culpability.

Partnership is about building a bridge half-way, then giving your partner the tools, materials and love (if they need them) to build the other half.

Love always takes courage, which is why a side effect of love is conquering fear. Have a wonderful day!

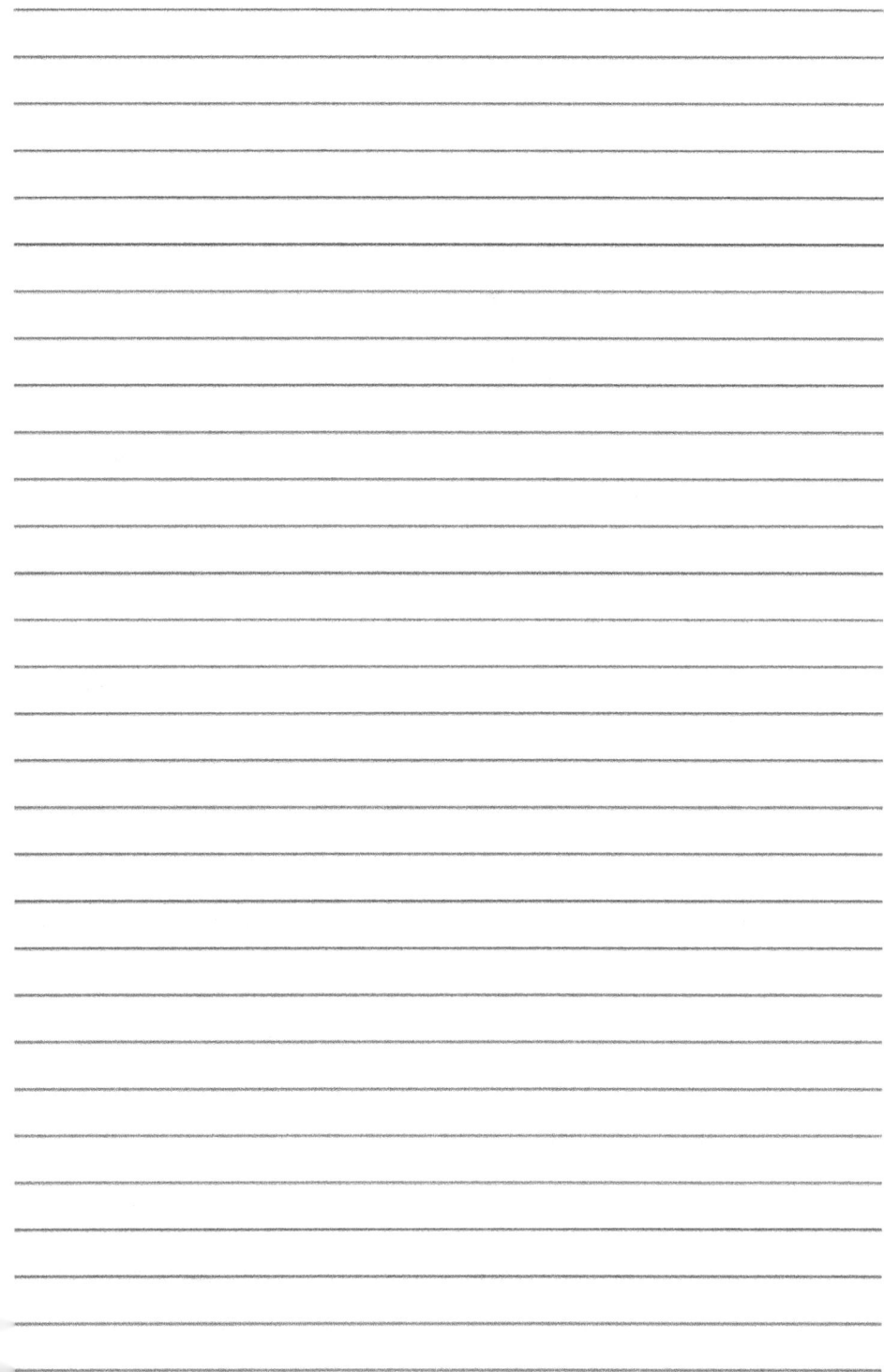

Fifth Day of the Week:

CONNECTION AND GIVING

Love Exercise Day 33

Take someone to lunch and ask open-ended questions about them. For example, "Tell me about some great things that happened in your life." Then tell them things that you loved about their story. Also, pay for lunch.

Journal.

The more you connect with people, the more they will connect with you (Love Secret #5). Though always give "the ball" first to the person with whom you want to connect. This person can be a stranger, someone you know well, or someone in-between the two. If it is someone you know well, ask a question that will result in learning something new. Make sure, when the opportunity comes, to open up about yourself.

Every human has the instinct to connect. This is a higher survival strategy and one of the elements of humanity's success as a species. If someone is reluctant to connect with you, you may need to build trust with them. Sometimes one's ability to connect has been somehow damaged or harmed. Sometimes a person can fear connection because previously it has meant pain or injury. In this case, healing and reactivating their love center needs to occur. Know that being interested in them while showing love and care can begin their healing process. If need be, open up about yourself to get "the ball" moving.

Bonus points for sharing dessert!

⊶ Sixth Day of the Week:

INNER SELF AND VISION

Love Exercise Day 34

Find a quiet place to sit undisturbed. Play your favorite love song. Listen very carefully to the lyrics, melody, rhythms, voice and instruments. Reflect on how all of the elements work together to create a single song. Repeat if necessary.

Journal.
Is there something in the song that resonates with what you want in life and love?

A masterpiece is a work of art in which all of its elements seamlessly work together to create a single, expressive wholeness. Masterpieces do not have to be elaborate or grandiose. Even a 3-minute song can be a masterpiece. As you listen to your favorite song, pay attention as to whether all of the elements are supporting each other. Is this song a masterpiece?

You are made up of many different components. When they all come together, supporting, enhancing, and resonating with each other, you begin to become a masterpiece. When your thoughts, emotions, attitudes, imagination, actions, and words are in alignment, each supporting your purpose, your wholeness and integrity begin to take form. Love is a means to get all of these elements resonating—getting them all on the same wavelength. Love will also take yourself to a higher vibration, which is easy to do when all of your parts are resonating as one.

You are a masterpiece!

♥ Seventh Day of the Week:

LOVE FREELY

Love Exercise Day 35

Pick one of the exercises from the past week to do over again. Add your own personal touch, variation or flavor if you wish. Or invent your own love exercise to do today and share it with our community.

Remember to journal!

Congratulations on completing 5 weeks! Have you heard that it takes 21 days to make a new habit? This idea comes from the book, *Psycho-Cybernetics* in which plastic surgeon, Dr. Maxwell Maltz claims that it took 21 days for new patients to create a new self-image of themselves after plastic surgery. This number soon came to be the standard amount of time in creating new habits.

New studies* have shown that some people take as little as 18 days to form new habits, and some take as long as 254 days. On average, it takes 66 days for a new habit to form. This is why I created *90 Days of Love* as opposed to 21 Days of Love. 90 days practically guarantees to create new habits of love. So no matter what, keep up this daily practice. Do not let yourself falter on such an important element of an amazing life that is love.

Love is the answer. And you get there by letting go of everything that gets in the way of love. Love has always been inside of you, maybe covered, hidden, or forgotten, but it has always been there.

Keep it up! See you tomorrow for Day 36.

*Lally, P., van Jaarsveld, C. H. M., Potts, H. W. W., & Wardle, J. (2010). How are habits formed: Modelling habit formation in the real world. European Journal of Social Psychology, 40, 998-1009. (http://onlinelibrary.wiley.com/doi/10.1002/ejsp.674/abstract)

Week 6 - Days 36-42

First Day of the Week:

I AM

Love Exercise Day 36

Look in the mirror for 5 minutes telling yourself, "I love you."

Journal.

I am a firm believer that everything you say to other people, you are really saying to yourself. So why not just talk to yourself directly? Seems like a good idea! Have fun with this exercise. Tell yourself "I love you" in as many different voices as you can come up with in 5 minutes. Be funny, sad, excited, goofy, outrageous, sexy, happy, etc. Put emphasis on each word individually. See what different meanings you can create. Stretch it out. Say it fast. Say it loud, proud, soft, scary, poetically, in a foreign accent.

See how amazing you are!

👤 Second Day of the Week:

BODY AND HEALTH

Love Exercise Day 37

Do a health inventory. List how often you are completely healthy, have no pain, exercise, and make healthy food choices. Now imagine yourself always being healthy, pain free, fit, and eating delicious, healthy food.

Journal.

As I said in the beginning, there are 5 Steps To Mastery: Intention, Knowledge, Practice, Feedback and Understanding. Checking in to your current status is a form of feedback. With this feedback, you are able to go back and revamp your steps starting with intention. Thus seeing your body as well-taken-care-of is a form of re-invigorating your intention for a healthy body. By re-connecting with your intention, you can seek new knowledge and practices to move you toward your vision.

Having a healthy body is not about measuring up to an ideal image. It is about loving and taking care of your body. Once you love your body, everything will get to where it wants to be.

This holds true for all four of your sides: physical, emotional, mental and spiritual.

Bonus points for checking in with your emotional, mental and spiritual sides!

_____

_____

_____

_____

_____

_____

_____

_____

_____

_____

_____

_____

_____

_____

_____

_____

_____

_____

_____

_____

Third Day of the Week:

ABUNDANCE

Love Exercise Day 38

Take a Love Walk. Go for a short 10-minute walk. While walking, as you look at what is around you, say to yourself, "I love this _____. I love that _____." For example, "I love this tree. I love that dog. I love this mailbox. I love that cloud."

When you get home, journal.

Your mind knows the meaning of the word "Love." So when you tell yourself that you love something, your mind knows how to feel. Your conscious tells your subconscious to create a feeling of connection for that object or animal.

Your experience of this exercise will depend on your experiences of love. In fact, it may reveal what is going on in your subconscious. In other words, this is an exercise that can create awareness of your beliefs regarding the experiences of love you have had in your past.

Regardless of your beliefs of love, this exercise will give you an experience of being present, in the moment, seeing the NOW. This is because saying, "I love ___" brings your attention to that thing or person, seeing it as it currently exists. Love has nothing to do with the past or future. Love is always in the moment. This is why love is the emotion of connection (Love Secret #2).

I put this exercise in the abundance category because it will always produce love. When you need love, this is an easy way to create it.

Don't worry about what people think of you. Be yourself. They will adjust!

Fourth Day of the Week:

POSITIVE EMOTIONS AND EXPRESSIONS

Love Exercise Day 39

Be honest with someone about your positive feelings for them.

Journal.

Before you are honest with someone, explain the context with them. Tell them your intention and reason for doing this exercise with them. For example, "I am doing a 90 day course on love and this is today's exercise." Or, "I am practicing being positive. May I practice with you?" Otherwise, people may assume a different intention, which can lead to disastrous results.

Bonus points for telling them what it means to you, or what it provides for you!

_____

_____

_____

_____

_____

Fifth Day of the Week:

CONNECTION AND GIVING

Love Exercise Day 40

Put $80 in your savings account. Give a random stranger $20.

Journal.

Money is never about what it can be exchanged for. Money is about security, power or experiences. I advocate having a savings account as an element of Partnership. This is because some agreements will be helped by having money on hand.

Money is like water to a plant. A plant needs water in many ways: to carry nutrients, provide building blocks for food, as well as structure and rigidity for the plant to function. Money does the same for you, but only if it is used, exchanged or given. As a farmer keeps a ready source of water, Partnerships keep a ready source of money.

At the same time, a farmer has to use the water they have in order to create abundance. So they are simultaneously saving water and using it. If they use all of their water, plants die. The same with your money. Always use less than you have.

Very short-term debt can be tolerated, but chronic long-term debt can be the death of a relationship.

What does this have to do with today's exercise? To give in a healthy way means to only give a percentage of what you have or else that part of you might never recover. This includes love, money, time, food, and everything else.

Can't wait to see the expression on their face!

_____

_____

_____

_____

_____

_____

_____

_____

_____

_____

_____

_____

_____

_____

_____

_____

_____

_____

OO Sixth Day of the Week:

INNER SELF AND VISION

Love Exercise Day 41

Find a quiet place to sit undisturbed. Relax. Breathe (6 seconds in, 6 seconds out.) Think of all the people with whom you had an experience of pain, grief, anger, misery, or resentment. See yourself forgiving and loving these people. See love growing inside of you.

Journal.

On Day 18, you worked to forgive yourself. Today, give the gift of forgiveness to others.

Today is about practicing letting go of the past. You cannot love while thinking of the past (or the future for that matter). Even if you are thinking of someone whom you loved in the past, you are not, at that moment, loving their current self.

Often times you are looking for answers when you just need to let go of the questions.

Holding on creates poison or toxins in the body and mind. Forgiveness clears this out. Forgiveness isn't about others. It's about you.

Connection is a continual process of updating. So as the Zen proverb states, "Let go or be dragged!"

♥ Seventh Day of the Week:

LOVE FREELY

Love Exercise Day 42

Pick one of the exercises from the past week to do over again. Add your own personal touch, variation or flavor if you wish. Or invent your own love exercise to do today and share it with our community.

Remember to journal!

Wow! 6 Weeks! Whew, you are amazing!

Think of the following quote as you create your loving day today.

"The grass isn't greener on the other side. The grass is greener where you water it. And the grass that is watered consistently and also fertilized is greenest of all."
- Gabrielle Reece and Karen Karbo. *My Foot Is Too Big For The Glass Slipper.* Pg. 173.

Just as watering and fertilizing soil will cause green, healthy grass to grow, accepting, forgiving, caring for, and loving yourself will cause connected, healthy relationships to grow in your life, including with yourself. Give yourself the needed nutrients for good things to flourish. Only you can let these good things into your being. You are the one that controls the doors to your heart. Now is the time to take a risk and open those doors wide open to the people in your life that you can trust, and perhaps have already been sending love your way.

I took this risk several times. Even though my heart was open, not every person chose to connect with me. And one time, I did get hurt. But like all of my hurts and wounds, physical or emotional, they heal quickly when I take care of myself. Then when an amazing, beautiful, caring woman did come into my life, I easily created trust with her and opened my heart. Love came pouring in, and love equally flowed out to her.

Given the right nutrients, Nature will grow green grass. Just as your Human Nature will grow love.

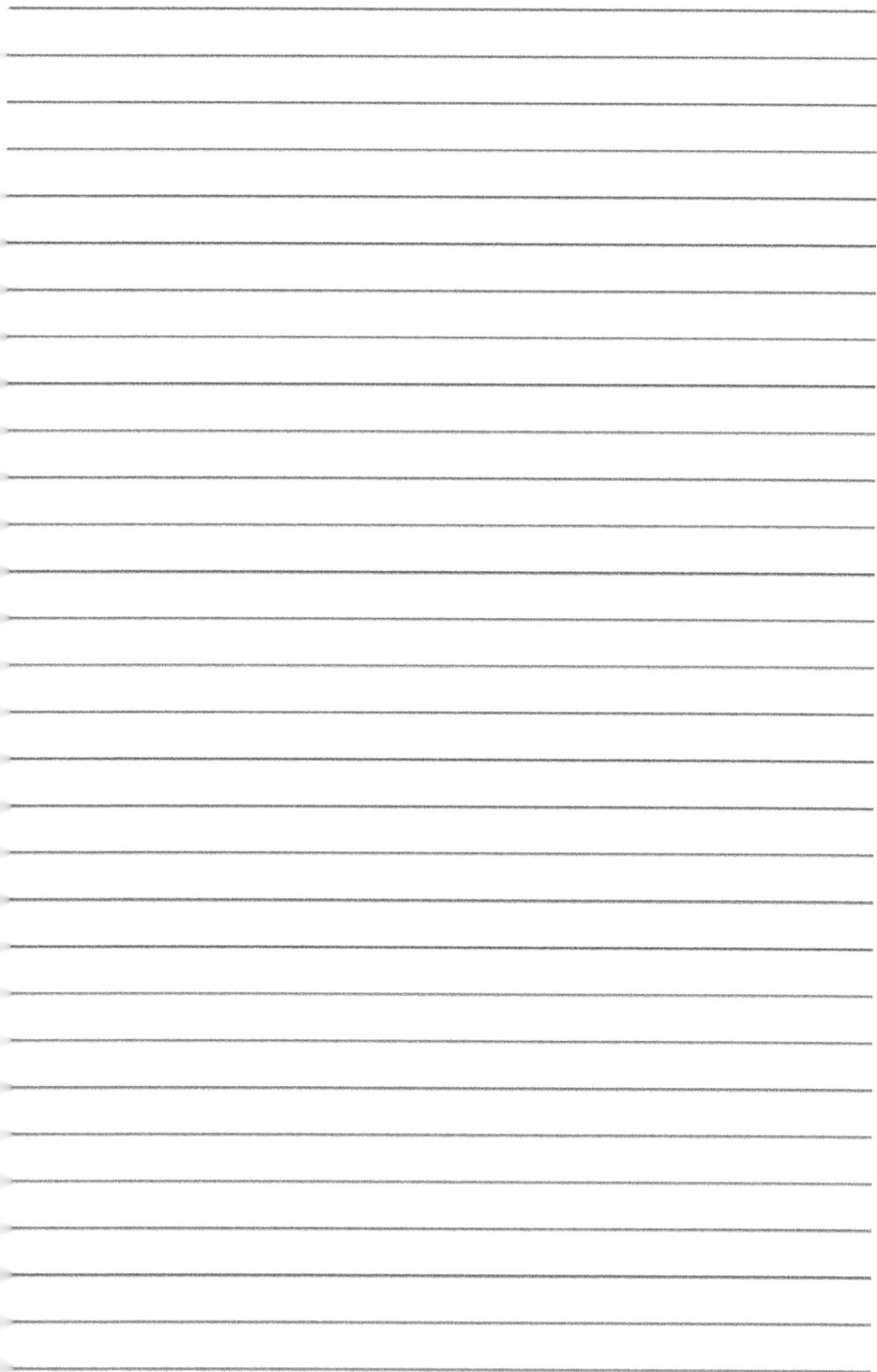

Week 7 - Days 43-49

👁 First Day of the Week:

I AM

Love Exercise Day 43

Look in the mirror for 5 minutes saying, "I love my hair. I love my eyes. I love my voice. I love my arms." Keep going, saying that you love every part of yourself including your mind, heart and spirit.

Journal.

You are a life form. You require nourishment. You need energy to grow, and that energy needs to be moving to be useful.

Love is energy that is put into motion by connection. Like all forms of energy, too little flow will hardly do any work, and too much flow can be destructive. So the best love is the kind that is moving like a peaceful river: abundant, consistent, full and life-giving.

Today is about keeping that energy flowing smoothly. Love is a daily, moment-by-moment endeavor. If you can create a habit of love—love without having to consciously think about it—all the better and easier for you to attract love into your life.

119

There is no such thing as redundant love!

Second Day of the Week:

BODY AND HEALTH

Love Exercise Day 44

Tell yourself, "I am committed to love." Do at least 5 minutes of intense exercise, repeating this statement to yourself out loud.

Journal.

This simple exercise is magic, for it has the power to blend together all four of your sides: physical, emotional, mental and spiritual. Saying "I am committed to love" out loud moves this powerful affirmation from your mind to your emotions. Saying it while exercising will move it to your body. Having it move throughout your mind, emotions, and body will help you to plant in into your spirit where it can take root and grow to maturity. When you think, feel, and embody commitment to love, you will be committed to love.

Whenever life has delivered a blow, or a person has pushed beyond your boundaries, or you are feeling crappy (which is your primitive brain's way to keep you safe), this is an effective, quick exercise to get you back on track. And it has the added bonus of burning a few calories, too!

121

You are worth creating love in every level of your life. This exercise will do just that!

_____

_____

_____

_____

_____

_____

_____

_____

_____

_____

_____

_____

_____

_____

_____

_____

_____

_____

_____

_____

_____

_____

Third Day of the Week:

ABUNDANCE

Love Exercise Day 45

Ask yourself, "What is my dream, purpose, or mission at this time in my life?" Write down your answer in your journal.

Continue to journal on who you need to be to make that dream come true.

I encourage you to take time working and thinking about today's exercise. This is important. This is your life. You don't have to have all of the answers at this moment. A good thing to do is to write in your journal until you run out of things to say.

If you feel stuck, or nothing is coming to you, then write down the first thing that comes to you, even if it is illogical, absurd, or something you have never thought of before. Or if fear is coming up for you, maybe this is the time to face that fear and put down the dream, purpose or mission you never before wanted to admit that you have.

Everything can be thought of as being created twice. The first instance of creation is when you have an intention for something, which in turn causes you to think about it. When your intention is big and life-changing, such as a dream, you automatically put your imagination into it, creating it perfectly in your mind.

The second instance of creation is when you take action on your intention. Since dreams are big, manifesting them usually takes many actions over long periods of time.

Today is about the first instance of creation. Take the time to create a perfect version of your dream, purpose or mission (or all three!) Get crystal clear on it. The clearer you are, the better chance it has of coming true.

You have all of my encouragement!

_____

_____

_____

_____

_____

_____

_____

_____

_____

_____

_____

_____

_____

_____

_____

_____

Halfway Check-In

Congratulations! You are half-way through *90 Days of Love*. Take some time today to look through your journal. It is a record of your journey. What were your obstacles? How did you move through them? The answer to these two questions can help point you to your purpose.

You may have noticed feelings, emotions and sensations in your body as you went through the exercises. Some of them may seem new. Some of them are probably not different than what you have felt before.

You may have had revelations and realizations about yourself, your perspectives and beliefs, and the world in general. Some of them may seem new. Some of them you already knew.

You may have seen yourself in a new light, new capabilities, new possibilities. You may be able to imagine being the person you had only dreamed of before. You may be ready to get there, or return there, or go beyond everything you have been and done previously.

A new you. This is what you've been working toward. What does this mean to you?

Hope turns into Faith. Faith turns into Certainty. Certainty turns into Reality.

Whether or not you have the exact results you wanted with *90 Days of Love*, never stop moving, never stop growing.

There is always more, and the journey is the greatest adventure.

Like Batman, it's a good idea to have a myriad of tools in your utility belt of love exercises. That way, for whatever comes your way, you will be able to pull out the one that will get you through your ordeal, or in comic book terms, capture the villain. If you think about it, after you have completed this course, you will have 90 tools at your disposal.

Pazow!

Fourth Day of the Week:

POSITIVE EMOTIONS AND EXPRESSIONS

Love Exercise Day 46

Make a list of people you do not like, putting next to their name one reason you do not like them. Then put something down that you <u>do</u> like about them.

Journal optional.

Every negative has a positive in it. And every positive has a negative in it. The universe is always moving toward balance. So have faith that your negatives have something positive to get out of it. At the same time, there is no need to extol your positives, for present in them is something negative.

To see people in a different way is to rewrite the story you have made up about them. Doing this will challenge how you see people and the world. By doing this exercise, you are changing your perspective.

You can change your perspective on yourself as well by rewriting your own stories. What you viewed as negative does have a positive, and vice versa. When you begin to see that negatives and positives are both opportunities for growing deeper in love, you will be in the place of unconditional love for yourself and for others.

Not many people have mastered unconditional love, but those few who did have made great and meaningful impacts on humanity.

It may take practice to find positives, but they are there.

🌉 Fifth Day of the Week:

CONNECTION AND GIVING

Love Exercise Day 47

Give up control of something you would normally control. If you need something done by someone else that you would normally tell or demand, make an agreement with that person. Ask them what they need to get the work done and give it to them.

Journal.

I introduced the 4 Pillars of Partnership on Day 28. One of those Pillars is Releasing Control. Today is about practicing this essential pillar. Why? Because Partnership cannot exist in the presence of control, and love is the result of Partnership.

Willard Harley, in his 25+ years of counseling couples, has seen over and over how fulfilling each other's needs through Partnership creates deeper and lasting connections between two people. In other words, practicing and maintaining a romantic Partnership creates love.

There are two more benefits of releasing control. First, you get to actually see what you have control over and where you have true power. Second, while attempts to control your external world can only take you to a certain level of success, Partnership agreements can take you beyond.

If you want things to turn out well, give up controlling everything!

-O-O- Sixth Day of the Week:

INNER SELF AND VISION

Love Exercise Day 48

Find a quiet place to sit undisturbed. Relax. Breathe. For 10 minutes, think of all the people who have loved you in your life. Imagine being them and loving you from their perspective. See love growing inside of you.

Journal.

There are two kinds of truth. The first kind is expressed in unbreakable laws and theories such as the Law of Gravity. If something is true throughout the universe, it is a law, whether you believe it or not.

The second kind of truth is expressed in terms of wholeness. Consider the following phrase:

Truth is the sum of all perspectives.

Today is about creating a new perspective of love for yourself through the eyes of those who love you. In this exercise, you have the opportunity to discover some more truths about yourself. Allow yourself to be open to what comes. Self-love means seeing yourself from all perspectives and accepting all of them.

Continue your day in this peaceful, relaxed state!

_____

_____

_____

_____

_____

_____

_____

_____

_____

_____

_____

_____

_____

_____

_____

_____

_____

_____

_____

_____

_____

_____

_____

_____

♥ ## Seventh Day of the Week:

LOVE FREELY

Love Exercise Day 49

Pick one of the exercises from the past week to do over again. Add your own personal touch, variation or flavor if you wish. Or invent your own love exercise to do today and share it with our community.

Remember to journal!

Love expands your world. Judgments shrink your world.

Often, the human mind fights against expansion, sending signals to your primitive brain to produce yucky feelings. This is a normal, human experience. But you have the awareness to keep loving no matter how you feel, for on the other side of love is a bigger world with more possibilities and opportunities.

So today, have a BIG day! Why? Because you have been expanding yourself for 7 weeks! It has probably been a roller coaster more than a car ride. But aren't roller coasters more fun!

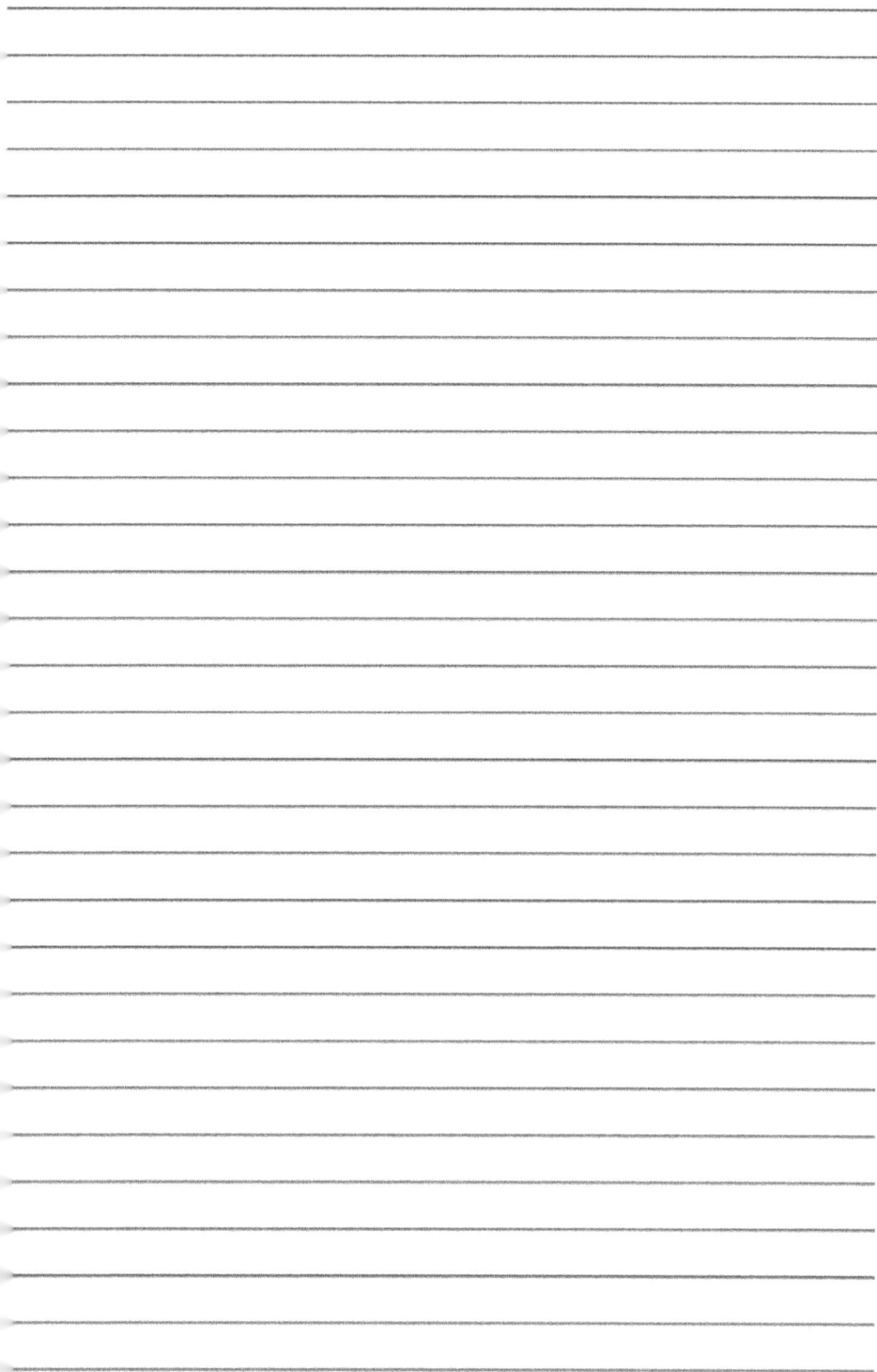

Week 8 - Days 50-56

First Day of the Week:

I AM

Love Exercise Day 50

Look in a mirror for 5 minutes saying, "I love my laughter. I love my intelligence. I love my imagination. I love my talents." Keep going through every part of your inner self and expressions.

Journal.

As I stated on Day 49, "Love expands your world, judgments shrink your world." This is true for your inner world as much as for your outer world. Some theoretical physicists think that the outer universe is infinite. One thing is for sure. The inner world is infinite. The only boundaries of the mind are the ones you put on it. This is one area of your life where you have complete control. The more you love your inner world, the more those boundaries will begin to dissolve.

Take your imagination beyond anything you've ever imagined before!

👤 Second Day of the Week:

BODY AND HEALTH

Love Exercise Day 51

Take a selfie of your entire body. Share it with friends with the tag, "I love my body!" Make a commitment to always take care of your body because you love it and are so very grateful for it.

Journal.

In almost all cases, any negative thought you have about your body comes from an outside source. For instance, friends or schoolmates made fun of the way you look, or made a negative comment on one of your features like your nose, hair, butt, feet, belly or anything. When this happened, you carried these comments with you for the rest of your life, or at least until you chose to believe something different, or when you began to lovingly accept yourself.

This happened to me. One day in high school, one of my best friends commented that I had an egg-shaped head. This stuck with me for the next three decades. So much so that when shaved-heads started becoming fashionable, though I wanted to do it, this belief about my head kept me from a good-looking haircut for over three years. Finally, with self-love and encouragement from my significant other, I broke through that belief.

The worst culprits of planting negative self-images into your subconscious are comments from family. Family is the place where love should dwell the strongest and brightest. But because it is also the place where you spend your formative years in vulnerability, you tend to soak up like a sponge things said about you, both positive and negative.

The good news is that through this course, you are creating a new commentary about yourself. Those old comments will always be there. But by having a new perspective, and not giving energy to those old beliefs, they will begin to go into hibernation, hopefully permanently.

When you have a strong heart, you get to choose what will get in and what can stay out.

Third Day of the Week:

ABUNDANCE

Love Exercise Day 52

Take another Love Walk. This time, as you see people from afar or close, say to yourself "I love (this person). I love (that person)." For example, "I love my neighbor. I love that man driving the truck."

Journal.

One of the best habits you can create for yourself is the habit of finding something to love about every person you know and meet. Not only will this create a connection, but it will also serve to remind you to love the person and not the deed.

In order for "All people are capable of love" to hold true, you must see people's bothersome behaviors as the result of inner beliefs and not of love. When you choose to love someone, you are searching for that part of them that wants connection. At the same time, through love, you are giving them a chance to become aware of their own limiting beliefs.

On the other hand, sometimes it is your own limiting beliefs that hold you back from connecting. Today's exercise is all about busting up those beliefs that prevent you from connecting with other people. And at the same time, influencing others to do the work to bust up their own beliefs.

When you hold each other to love, peace finds a home.

Fourth Day of the Week:

POSITIVE EMOTIONS AND EXPRESSIONS

Love Exercise Day 53

If you feel negative about someone, be honest with yourself about why. Most likely, it is because of something you do not like about yourself.

Journal.

If you are having trouble pinpointing your exact limiting beliefs, today's exercise is the best way to expose them. Be willing to do the work and examine your thoughts. Dig deep into yourself. It's OK to have things that you do not like about yourself. It's not OK to let them get in the way of love and connection.

On Day 6, I explained how the mind projects your perceptions onto the outside world. Looking at this concept in reverse, the mind can be thought of as a filter, only allowing you to see those parts of the outer world that fit your beliefs. Thus what you see in other people will be in alignment with your own beliefs. Examine what you do not like about people, and you will be able to see that there is a personal belief behind your annoyance.

For instance, one day I joked to a couple about the wife never letting her husband get a word in edgewise. That couple did not think it was funny. At that moment, I took the time to do the hard work and ask myself why this couple annoyed me. And it was this. I had observed how much the wife loved and respected her husband and I did not believe that such love was possible. From that time forward, I chose to accept that women do love and respect men very much. This change in perspective changed my life!

I do concede that it took months for me to change my personal belief that I was lovable. Although becoming aware of this belief was instant, using the 5 steps to mastery, I put in the work and practice to realize that a woman could love and respect me.

Do the work today and everyday! It is worth it.

Fifth Day of the Week:

CONNECTION AND GIVING

Love Exercise Day 54

Spend time with someone who deserves your time.

Journal.

What you put energy into, grows.

Because you are willing to give time to someone who truly deserves your time, you are giving them life in the form of a positive experience with you. Humans are experiential beings, meaning we crave adventure, new events, overcoming challenges and excitement.

So when you spend time with your special person today, give them a meaningful experience of connection on a whole new level. If necessary, be willing to break through fear to see what happens. Connection promotes growth when both people come from authenticity—extreme honesty. Authenticity also means acknowledging to your special person that you want to connect, and it may be scary for you. Your special person will respect that.

Love is giving energy, and vice versa!

⊙⊙ Sixth Day of the Week:

INNER SELF AND VISION

Love Exercise Day 55

Find a quiet place to sit undisturbed. Relax. Breathe. Think of one person whom you always try to avoid. See yourself sending beams of love to them. See them being amazing in their life.

Journal.

Today's exercise is based on a success tool in the book, *The Tools*, by Phil Stutz and Barry Michels. The tool is called Active Love.

Do you believe you can influence other people with this tool? If not, do it and find out. If so, by all means use it! If anything, you will end up influencing yourself.

The personal benefit of sending love can often be greater than the beneficial effect on the receiver. Sending someone love means you have to open your heart to them. The more you do this, the more likely your heart will have a continuous open channel for connection.

Beam me up!

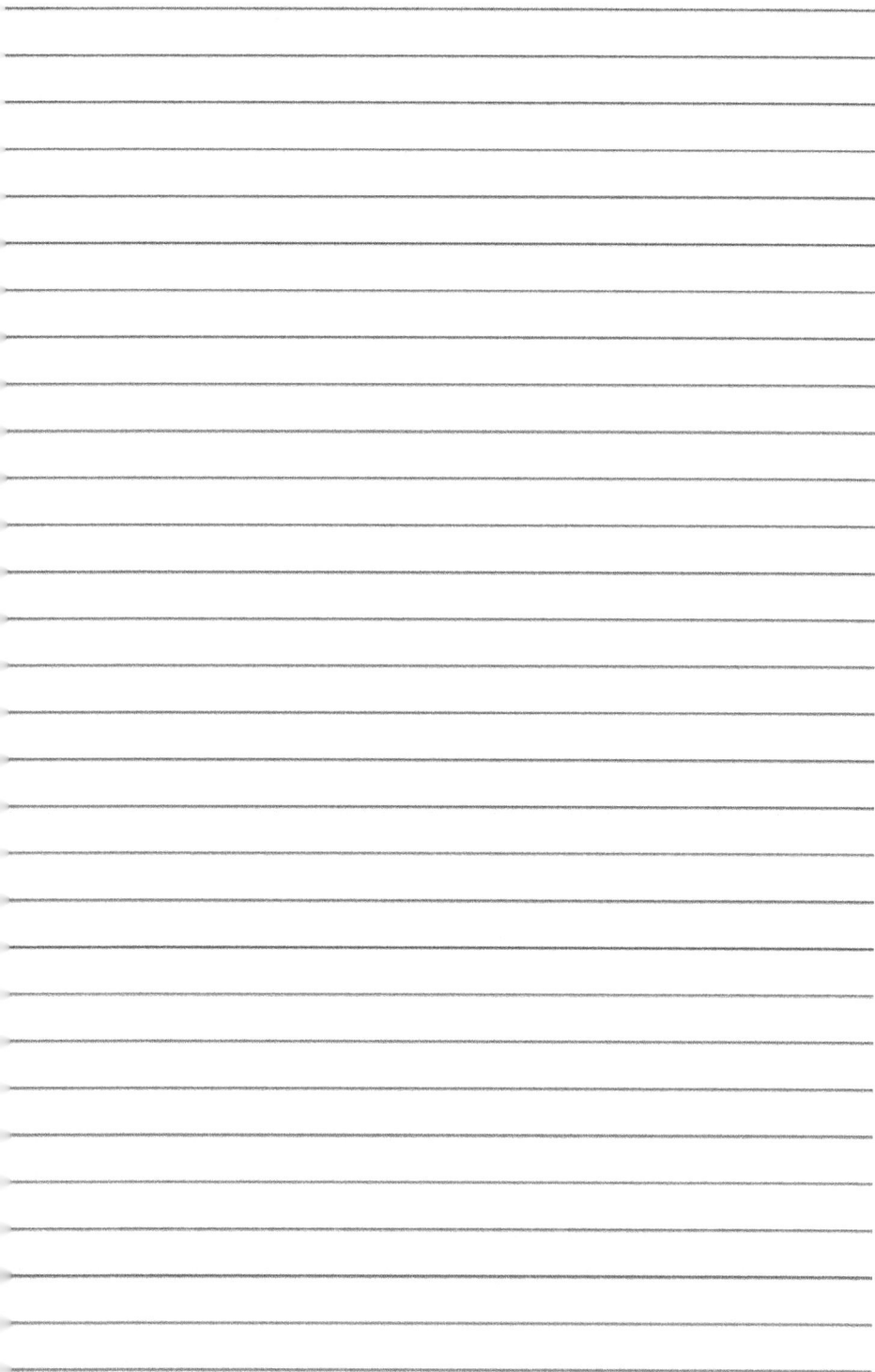

♥ Seventh Day of the Week:

LOVE FREELY

Love Exercise Day 56

Pick one of the exercises from the past week to do over again. Add your own personal touch, variation or flavor if you wish. Or invent your own love exercise to do today and share it with our community.

Remember to journal!

Hopefully I have established that love is synonymous with connection. And love is part of a larger system of one-ness. Anytime you connect with another person on any level, whether physically, emotionally, mentally or spiritually, unity is felt. And hopefully there's a realization is that you are part of this universe.

The word "universe" comes from "uni" meaning "one", and "versus" meaning "toward." Together it means "combined into one whole."

If you want to see the universe, just open your eyes!

Congratulations on 2 months of love exercises! I am so happy for you!

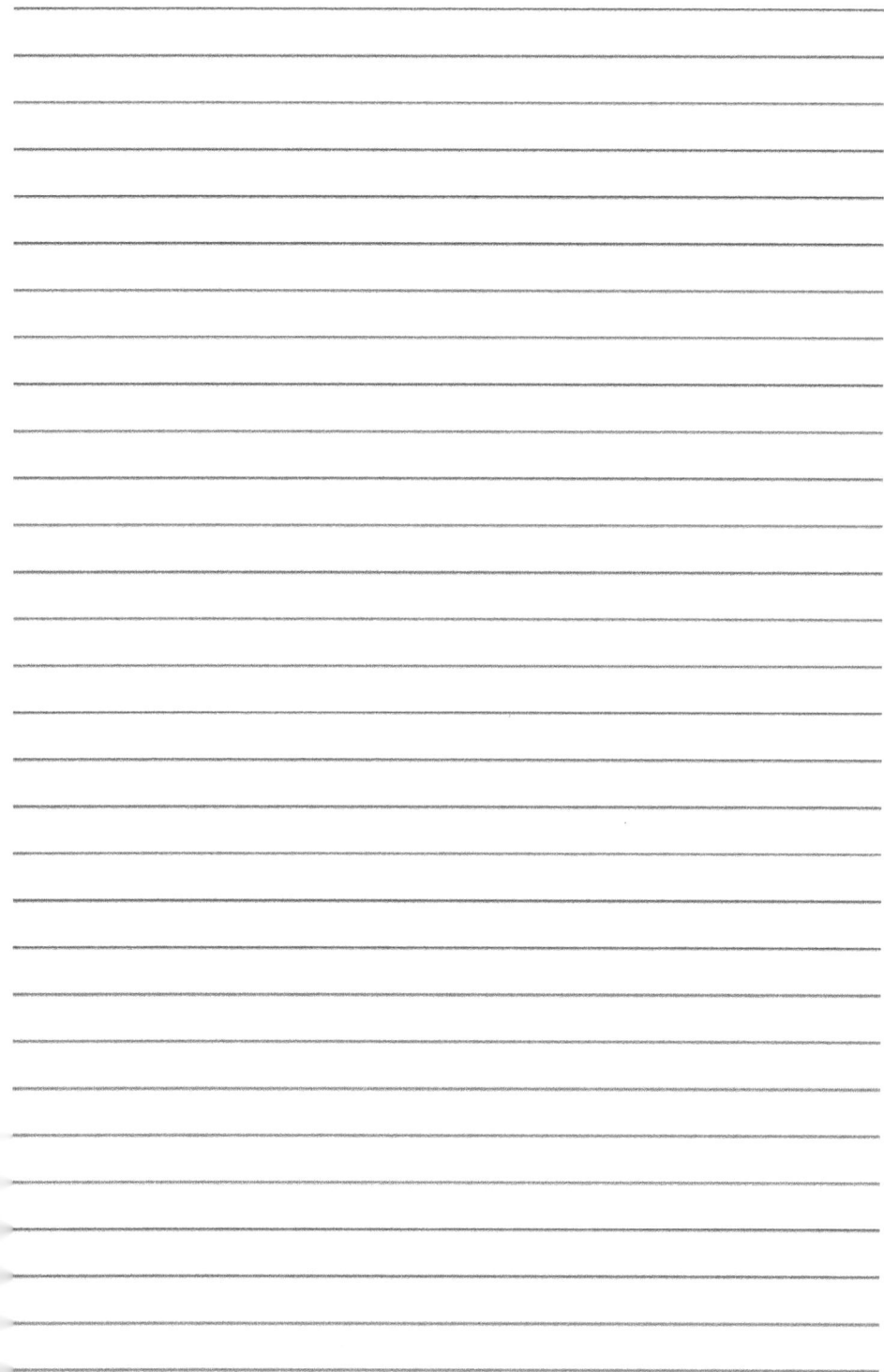

Week 9 - Days 57-63

First Day of the Week:

I AM

Love Exercise Day 57

For 5 minutes, look in a mirror and tell yourself, "You are amazing. You are sexy. You are smart. You are capable. You are worthy. You are loved. You are loving." Keep going with more affirmations of how you want to be.

Journal.

Every one of these attributes and qualities are within you. In fact, you were born with them.

90 Days of Love is not about creating love directly, so to speak, but about creating a healthy soil where love will thrive. All you have to do is plant the seeds!

Today is about fertilizing your soil; giving yourself all the nutrients that love needs to grow. You are a being that is born to connect. For all of your life, you will need the nutrients that are going to support you in connecting with other people. Start by giving them to yourself. And, once your "love nutrients" are in abundance, you will be able to give them freely to other people.

Saying "You are . . . " to yourself is a step towards saying "I am . . . " If you are comfortable saying "I am amazing. I am sexy" and so forth, by all means do that.

If you are not comfortable saying "I am . . . " then this at least will get you the practice of directing your thoughts to self-love. There is an "I am . . . " exercise in the weeks to come.

You are a fertile field for love to grow!

👤 Second Day of the Week:

BODY AND HEALTH

Love Exercise Day 58

Make plans to go out tonight and have fun. For instance, go to your favorite restaurant with a friend or significant other. Get dressed up! Have a great time and thank your body for the fun.

Journal.

You are not mind and body and spirit, just as a car is not steering and engine and gas. Yes these are components, but truly you are a single entity: mind-body-spirit. And more so, you are one piece of the puzzle of connected humanity which is one piece of the biggest puzzle of all: the universe. By taking care of your body, you are also taking care of your mind and spirit, and through connection, other people and the universe.

Fun is a celebration of connection. So as you have fun tonight, enjoying your mind-body-spirit, take a moment to understand how many other mind-body-spirits you are celebrating. Understand how this in turn takes care of greater things.

153

When you spend money to have fun, you are supporting thousands of other people. By going out to dinner, you are supporting all the restaurant staff, the utility people who supply electricity, water and gas, the road crews who repair roads, the banking people who put up capital, the food distributors, farmers and all of those supporting industries, delivery people, website programmers who build the restaurant's websites, etc. You get the picture. In turn, know that thousands of people have to spend money to support you. In truth, the economy is a form of connection.

Love the economy and it will love you in return.

Third Day of the Week:

ABUNDANCE

Love Exercise Day 59

Think of your big dream. Then think of two people you know personally. Go to lunch or coffee together and tell them your dream.

Afterwards, journal. Include their reactions and your response to them.

First, you need to make a distinction between goals and dreams. Goals are S.M.A.R.T. That is: specific, measurable, attainable, risky and have a time to be achieved. At this time, if your dream cannot fit into the criteria of becoming a goal, don't worry about it. At some future time, it may be!

Second, you need to make a distinction between big and small dreams. If you can make your dream come true on your own, your dream is not big enough. You will know your dream is big when you need support to bring it to reality.

Saying your dream out loud to others is a big boost for self-love, no matter how other people respond. Love is one of the internal power sources that will fuel your dreams into becoming reality. The other two are desire and faith. When

155

you have all three, you truly have rocket fuel. Since you have
been putting all of this work in creating love within yourself,
now it is time to put that love to work.

Fourth Day of the Week:

POSITIVE EMOTIONS AND EXPRESSIONS

Love Exercise Day 60

Think of someone you know who could use more love in his or her life. Inspire them to take their own journey into creating more love for themselves.

Journal.

You are influential. True! Today, while doing this exercise, think in the back of your mind how you are influencing people. Is it in a good way? Is it in a bad way? Is it in an inspirational way?

Here is the origin of the word inspire.

From the Latin *inspirare* "breathe" or "blow into" from *in* - "into" + *spirare* - "breathe." The word was originally used in reference to divinity entering a person, in the sense of imparting life, a truth or idea to someone. (From the New Oxford American Dictionary)

If you take "breath" as life-force, "inspire" literally means "to put life into someone through a truth or an idea."

Inspiring someone is a form of unconditional giving, which is a form of love. So today is about using love to go beyond influential and into inspiring.

You can fan the flames of love!

Fifth Day of the Week:

CONNECTION AND GIVING

Love Exercise Day 61

Collect money for a charity. Donate the money anonymously.

Journal.

Today is about experiencing Love Secret #5, "The more you connect with people, the more they will connect with you," but in a slightly different form.

For as you care for others, others will care for you.

This does not mean that the same "others" will take care of you, but that a new group of people will be there to support you when you need support. This exercise is about cementing in your mind the truth that there will always be people to catch you when you fall. You will know this truth because of the fact that you were there to help catch people when they fell.

If you are already active in collecting and donating to charities, make sure as you do this today that you are coming from the perspective of creating inner peace as well as outer peace. Your inner peace will be from knowing that though you may fail, you will not fall.

To be strong and still put others first is a sign of nobility.

⟋⟍ Sixth Day of the Week:

INNER SELF AND VISION

Love Exercise Day 62

Find a quiet place to sit undisturbed. Relax. Breathe. Think about the one person you love above all others. See yourself loving all others this same amount, including yourself. Visualize love growing inside of you.

Journal.

Today's exercise is a ramping-up of the similar exercise from Day 13. Though instead of meditating on what love feels like for you, which was Day 13's exercise, today is about recreating your greatest love.

I have already stated that you were born with the ability to connect deeply with others. At some point in your life, this ability revealed itself. With this course, *90 Days of Love*, you are tapping into this natural ability, becoming aware of how it works, and using it so that you can connect with people at will.

The goal is to create connection and love with everyone you know with the same degree you have for those special people you deeply love. Today is about envisioning this goal so you can make it a reality.

Happy meditating!

♥ Seventh Day of the Week:

LOVE FREELY

Love Exercise Day 63

Pick one of the exercises from the past week to do over again. Add your own personal touch, variation or flavor if you wish. Or invent your own love exercise to do today and share it with our community.

Remember to journal!

"Controlling life rather than trusting life is never the answer; it's always the problem."
- Joseph J. Luciani, Ph.D. *Reconnecting: A Self-Coaching Solution to Revive Your Love Life.* Pg. 133.

Sometimes letting your outer life happen, as opposed to controlling it, gets you to a new and better place. This is the meaning of the above quote. This is also true for your inner life. Allowing your feelings to happen rather than controlling them will get you to a new and better place.

You can practice this using The Pause. The Pause is the time between your reaction and your response. A reaction is an immediate emotional event. It could be considered emotional chaos. When you react to an external trigger, do your best to Pause, waiting before you say or do anything.

Internally, your thoughts and feelings are going through chaos, but if you wait long enough, you finally get your conscious thinking back and can respond with love.

At the suggestion of a friend, I started using this practice to startling success. By Pausing after an emotional reaction, I have been able to respond with love and curiosity instead of resentment or anger. I have since read about The Pause in several books including *Loving Bravely* by Alexandra H. Solomon, Ph.D. and *The Power of Losing Control* by Joe Caruso.

Let the chaos happen! And Congrats on 9 weeks! 4 weeks to go!

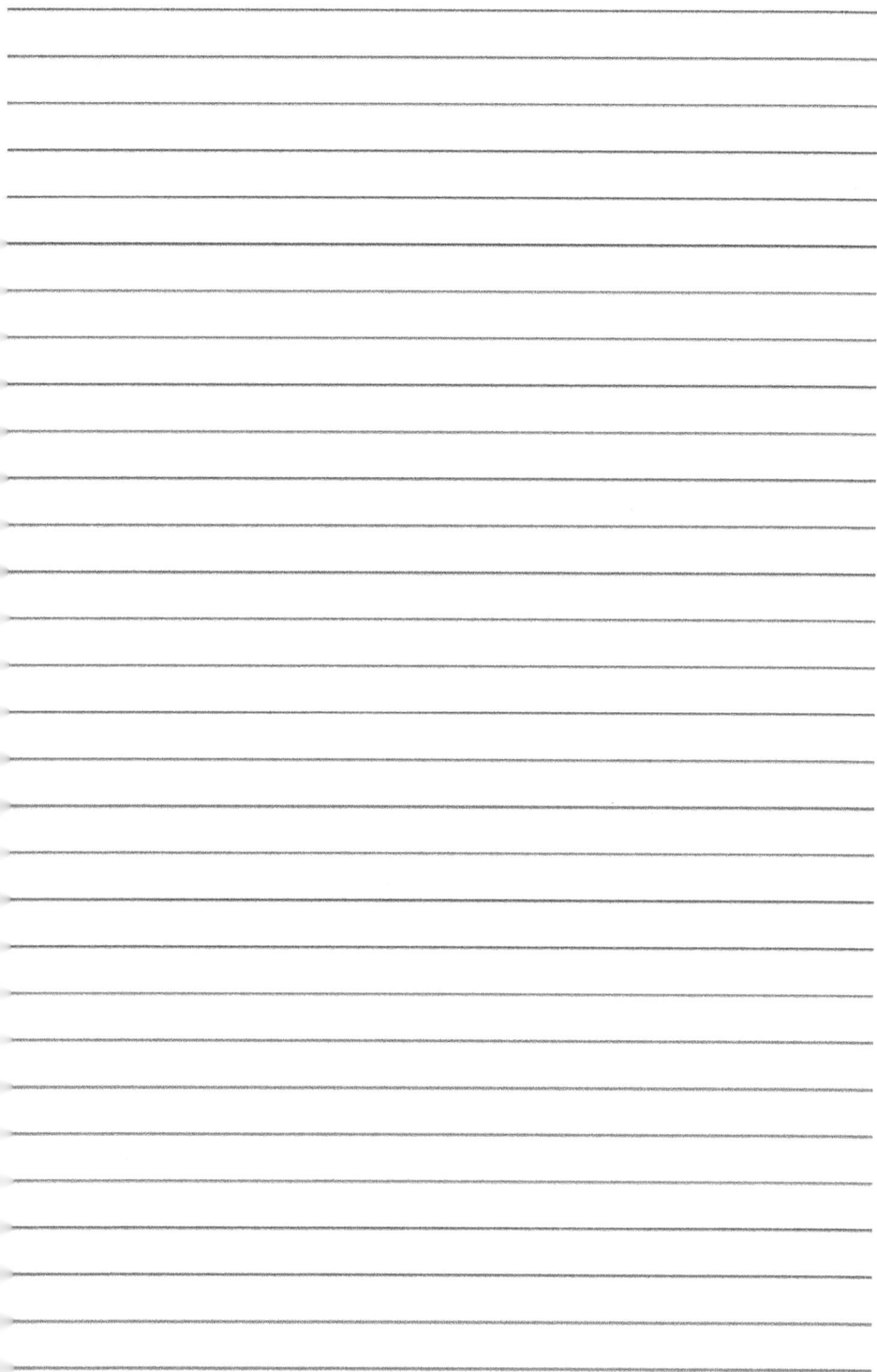

Week 10 - Days 64-70

First Day of the Week:

I AM

Love Exercise Day 64

Look in a mirror for 5 minutes without saying anything. At the end of 5 minutes, describe out loud how you feel about yourself.

Journal.

Only you know your own truth. But at the same time, everyone else can tell if you are being authentic. Authenticity is when your feelings, thoughts and behaviors align with your own truth.

People have a funny sort of radar that can detect authenticity and phoniness. You have it too. Even people who act phony have this radar. They either don't know, or they deny that people can tell they are being phony. Other people don't trust what this radar is telling them, so they ignore the messages and end up following phony people to their own detriment.

Today is about trusting yourself to be authentic. When you are being authentic, your "authenticity radar" becomes hyper sensitive. You are able to see people's phoniness just as plain as you see them with your eyes. The same goes when you look in the mirror for 5 minutes without saying anything.

The best way to love someone who is acting phony is to call him or her on it. That's all. Then let them acknowledge it or not. If they acknowledge it, it's possible that connection will occur.

Also, have you noticed how gorgeous your eyes are?

Second Day of the Week:

BODY AND HEALTH

Love Exercise Day 65

For five minutes, tell yourself, "Today I am committed to love my body unconditionally and I surrender to what my body is telling me." Write this exact sentence in your journal.

Continue to journal.

Your body-mind-spirit is always telling you what you need. An aspect of self-love is listening to yourself and giving yourself what you need, unconditionally. The second part of the above commitment statement has to do with surrender. In this case, surrender is the opposite of resistance. Once you hear what your body-mind-spirit is telling you, do not resist the message.

Surrender is most often thought of as an act of giving up, as during a battle. But surrender means giving-in. Even though a soldier might surrender, or give-in to losing a battle, he or she certainly hasn't given up on winning. So today, make the commitment to always listen to your mind-body-spirit. For this is how you will be able to love yourself.

Watch the movie, *Embrace*, about Taryn Brumfitt's journey to inspire everyone, especially women, to embrace their bodies. This movie is the inspiration for Day 51 and today's love exercises.

Never give up!

Third Day of the Week:

ABUNDANCE

Love Exercise Day 66

Make a list of the people who <u>could</u> support your dreams.
Make a list of the people who <u>would</u> support your dreams.
Next to each person, list what you think they need from
you to support your dreams.

Journal optional.

The ability to connect with people is the key to making your big dreams into big goals. Big goals can only be achieved through relationships. As I said before, love is the flow of energy generated through connection. That flowing energy can fuel the realization of your dreams into goals. This is one of the reasons I developed *90 Days of Love*—for you to fulfill a big dream, such as having a daily, rewarding, extraordinary relationship with the love of your life!

Have you heard of win-win? This is creating a relationship where both people are winning. If in the process of making your dream come true, other people's dreams are supported, it's a win-win situation. Win-win is how Partnerships operate, one reason why they always lead to abundance.

171

Today's exercise is about imagining how to make a win-win relationship with the people who can support your dreams. Give this some time, energy and thought. It could change the trajectory of your life.

_____
_____
_____
_____
_____
_____
_____
_____
_____
_____
_____
_____
_____
_____
_____
_____
_____
_____
_____
_____
_____

Fourth Day of the Week:

POSITIVE EMOTIONS AND EXPRESSIONS

Love Exercise Day 67

In your journal, keep a list of all the emotions you feel today. At the end of the day, separate them into ones that worked for you and ones that did not work.

Journaling optional.

First, if you have trouble identifying emotions, here is a website with a good chart that you can use. https://www.simplemost.com/feeling-wheel-will-help-better-describe-emotions/

Here is a perspective on the effectiveness of emotions in your life. Every emotion at some time is effective and at some time is not effective, including love. Maybe read this twice. Sometimes love is not the most effective emotion. The trick with emotions is to switch to a different one when the current one is not working. "How do I switch emotions?" you may ask. The first step to switching emotions is to be able to acknowledge the one you are currently experiencing. Once you acknowledge an emotion, your conscious can take it over and direct it. The second step is to have a repertoire of go-to emotions. Today's exercise is to get you started in both of these steps.

Here's another question you may ask. "Love is not always effective? Why not?" You will come across people to which connection is a scary or uncomfortable thing. Yes, love will open them up, but before that, they may put up big walls and have their defenses in full attack mode. This is where another emotion besides love may work better to get them to put their defenses down enough to spark a connection.

In the steps to mastery, today is about the fourth step, feedback. Taking a look at yourself brings you another step closer to becoming a Master of Love.

Fifth Day of the Week:

CONNECTION AND GIVING

Love Exercise Day 68

Give a $20 (or more) food gift card to a homeless person or someone who needs it more than you.

Journal.

First of all, if it is unsafe for you to approach a homeless person, please at least give the $20 to someone who could use a helping hand.

Although this is not a permanent solution for a homeless person's predicament, it at least demonstrates that someone cares. While doing this, it is important to distinguish motivations. For instance, giving because of care for the person as opposed to alleviating guilt for having more, or because it's the right thing to do.

If you have guilt for being better off than other people, then you have an internal belief that you do not deserve the things you have. The truth is that at some level you have taken responsibility for your life and for this you need to thank yourself. If you were given the resources to be better off, then be in gratitude. Isn't it true that you built yourself with your gifts rather than completely destroy yourself?

If you think that this is the right thing to do, see that there is a possibility that this is not the right thing to do. You never know how a person is going to receive a gift of food. And neither can you control how they will receive it.

So why do it? Because it at least is an opportunity for that person to realize that people do care about them, and that if they can do a little better, we all do a little better as well.

Bonus points for connecting with them!

-O-O- Sixth Day of the Week:

INNER SELF AND VISION

Love Exercise Day 69

Find a quiet place to sit undisturbed. Relax. Breathe. Think of your life if every interaction with every person you ever come across is one of unconditional love. See love growing inside of you.

Journal.

Though unconditional means "not subject to any conditions," Unconditional Love has a different meaning to each person. What does it mean for you? What do you think it means for your loved ones?

_____

_____

_____

_____

_____

_____

_____

_____

_____

_____

_____

♥ Seventh Day of the Week:

LOVE FREELY

Love Exercise Day 70

Pick one of the exercises from the past week to do over again. Add your own personal touch, variation or flavor if you wish. Or invent your own love exercise to do today and share it with our community.

Remember to journal!

As with all journeys of learning, one has to start out simple and gradually add difficulty with challenges to practice, overcome and master. *90 Days of Love* is no exception. I have been incrementally making each day a little more demanding in order to work and stimulate your love center.

Maybe some days have been easy for you, which is perfectly fine. Perhaps other days have been quite a stretch. That is great, too. If you are able to expand yourself even a little bit, your love center will become more active and stronger. That is the goal!

Love is infinite. Not only can love never run out, there are infinite ways to love.

Congratulations on 10 amazing weeks!

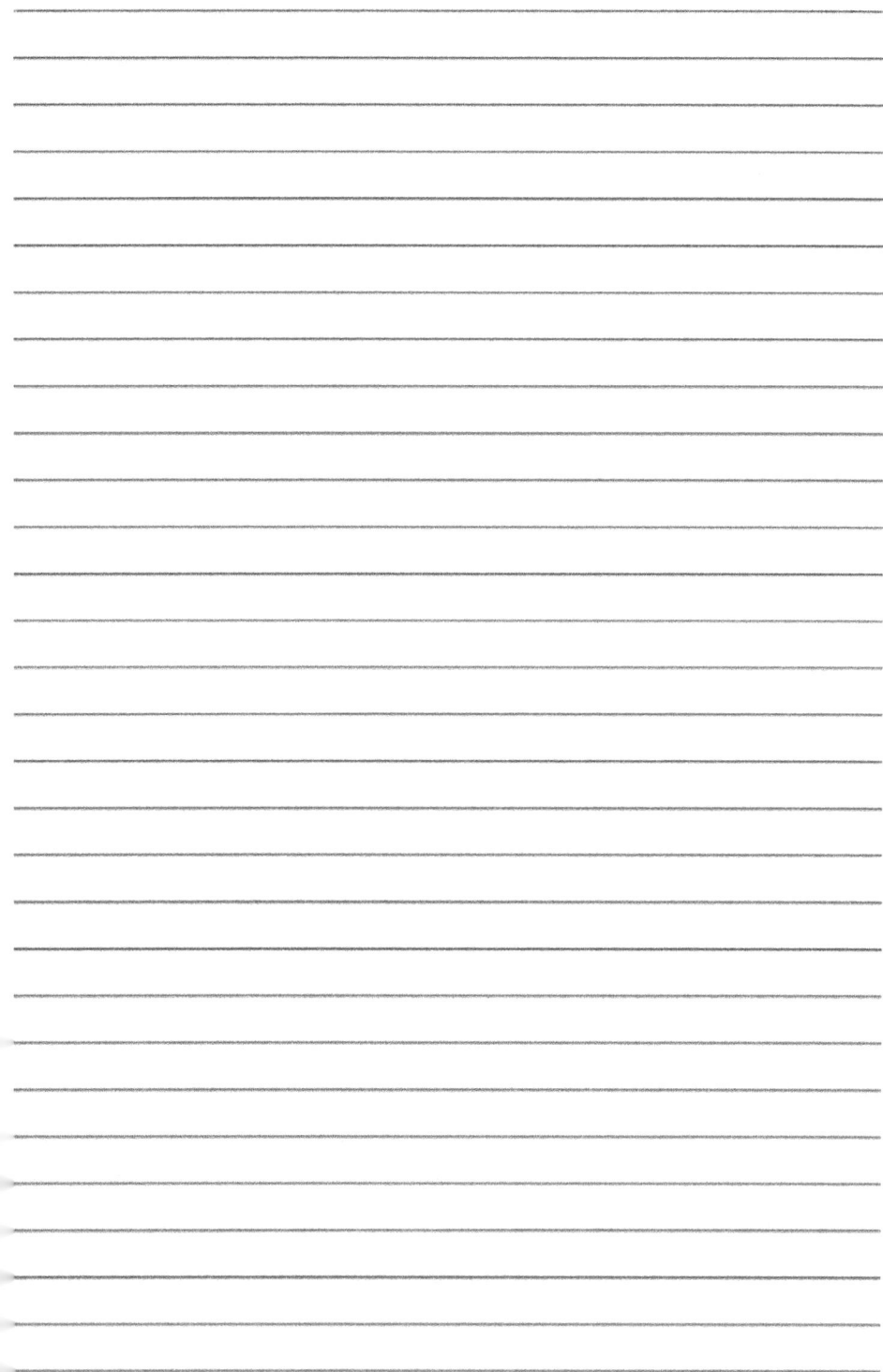

Week 11 - Days 71-77

First Day of the Week:

I AM

Love Exercise Day 71

Before you do this exercise, read your journal from Day 64.

Look in a mirror for 5 minutes, completely naked. If there is a negative feeling about any part of yourself, look at that part very intensely and in detail. Tell yourself that you love every inch of that part of your body.

Journal.

What did you feel about yourself during that exercise? Now answer this: Did you choose how you felt or did you let your subconscious decide?

Today, you get an opportunity to choose how you feel about yourself. If you choose not to love every inch of your body, what are you choosing to feel about it? You are in control of yourself—if you decide to take control. I said earlier that no person can control another person (2nd Law of Love.) But indeed, you can control yourself. To do this, you must first decide that you are fully responsible for everything in your life, including the amount of love that flows through you.

You are responsible for your own love! You may not realize it now, but there is tremendous power in this knowledge.

Second Day of the Week:

BODY AND HEALTH

Love Exercise Day 72

Have a Relaxing Day. Thank your body by giving it a long, hot bath, shower, or the thing that works to relax you. Then find a nice place to rest for a few hours. Leave all of your worries behind. Allow your body to re-energize.

Journal.

On Day 23, I explained the difference between "deserve" and "earn." After 71 days of love exercises, you certainly have both earned and deserve a Relaxing Day. On top of this, let today be about recharging your batteries. But before you allow love to pour into your body, make sure all of your energy holes are patched up. If need be, take a Love Walk, or do a Love Meditation, or connect with someone who loves you unconditionally. Sit back and say goodbye to all of your worries while you visualize the white light of love filling you up to the brim.

While resting, imagine every day of your life being a Relaxing Day. Not that it would necessarily include a long, hot bath or shower, or resting for a few hours, but that it would be about leaving your worries behind, keeping your body in a relaxed state, having a clear, peaceful mind, and creating more internal energy than you use. One way to make this a reality is to follow your dream, as long as your dream reflects your most important values. When you choose to live your life how you want and create a circle of loving family, friends and colleagues, you will live an inspired, enthusiastic, relaxing life full of energy.

Let love come in! Let love go out!

Third Day of the Week:

ABUNDANCE

Love Exercise Day 73

Pick one person from your list on Day 66. Contact them and have a conversation about how they can support your dream. If they can, ask them what they want and need from you. Make an agreement.

Journal.

Today is about taking action.

On Day 45, I talked about everything being created twice, the first time in the imagination, the second time in reality. Today is about taking action on your dream—bringing it to reality. As you may recall from Day 20, the most important step is always the next step. This is the next step.

Even if your dream cannot be made into a goal at this time, love for yourself, and by proxy, your dream, purpose, or mission, will create passion that comes across to people. When you connect with people who can support your dream, this passion is what they will be looking for. Use your growing love to conquer any fears that prevent the expression of your dream in the most passionate terms and emotions. Even if you can only connect by email or text,

185

true passion will still come through. Love is an amazing transformational energy, and the source of it is infinite. So use it!

Make sure you journal your internal dialogue before and after you contact your support person. Was it positive, negative, neutral? Did it bring up the past? If it did bring up the past, remember that love brings you into the NOW. While in a state of love, there is no past and you can easily move toward the future you want.

Go for it!

Fourth Day of the Week:

POSITIVE EMOTIONS AND EXPRESSIONS

Love Exercise Day 74

From your list on Day 46, pick the one person who bothers you the most. Contact them and tell them one thing you like about them. Ask them about their life. Be interested.

Journal.

Today in essence is about practice—the 3rd step in mastery.

On Day 53, I asked you to examine your beliefs that lead to dislikes and annoyances. Today is about shifting perspectives, specifically shifting from your perspective to their perspective. See the world through their eyes. Or, as the saying goes, stand in their shoes. What do you think motivates their behaviors?

Entertain the possibility that both of your perspectives are valid. Or put differently, see the possibility that both of you are right.

Truth is the sum of all perspectives (See Day 48). Unfortunately, each of us individually can only see the truth from our own perspective. But you can expand upon what you see by accepting that what others see is just as real, valid and right.

Bonus points for getting feedback!

_____

_____

_____

_____

_____

_____

_____

_____

_____

_____

_____

_____

_____

_____

_____

_____

_____

_____

_____

_____

_____

_____

_____

Fifth Day of the Week:

CONNECTION AND GIVING

Love Exercise Day 75

Ask 3 people, "What is your dream, purpose, or mission?" If they give you an answer, ask them, "How can I support you?" If you need something from them to support them, let them know.

Write down their answers in your journal.

Today is an extension of yesterday's exercise of learning about other people from their perspective. But more so, it is a lesson about support.

Loving people does not mean you have to completely support them. First of all, supporting everyone you love is impossible. So don't do it. Love requires honesty about what you can do and cannot do. Anytime you are sacrificing your well-being, you are losing and this is not a form of love.

If you ask someone, "How can I support you?" and they answer, you have choices in your response.

1. Yes, I can do that and I do not need anything from you.

2. Yes, I can do that and I need _____ from you.

3. No, I cannot do that, but I can help you find someone who can do that.

4. No, I cannot do that.

Answers 1-3 will create connection and love. Answer 4 means that a solution hasn't yet been found.

The important thing to know is that creating boundaries is a form of love, as long as they are honest and authentic to who you are and what you need.

Have a happy day!

Sixth Day of the Week:

INNER SELF AND VISION

Love Exercise Day 76

Find a quiet place to sit undisturbed. Relax. Breathe.
Think of the source of love. Where does it come from?
How can you get more of it to flow into you? Envision love
growing inside of you.

Journal.

Some people are easy to love. Some people are difficult to love.

Love from afar is easy. Love close up is difficult.

Loving those who are similar to you is easy. Loving those who are different from you is difficult.

Loving people who are nice is easy. Loving people who are mean is difficult.

Loving people who belong to your group is easy. Loving people who do not belong to your group is difficult.

Loving some people is easy. Loving all people is difficult.

When and where do you need more love?

♥ # Seventh Day of the Week:

LOVE FREELY

Love Exercise Day 77

Pick one of the exercises from the past week to do over again. Add your own personal touch, variation or flavor if you wish. Or invent your own love exercise to do today and share it with our community.

Remember to journal!

Congratulations on making it eleven weeks! Are you beginning to understand The Five Secrets of Love? Here they are again:

#1 You are capable of realizing your dreams of love.

#2 Love is the emotion of connection.

#3 You are able to consciously create love.

#4 Your thoughts and behaviors affect your love.

#5 The more you connect with people, the more they will connect with you.

As a reminder here are also the 5 Steps to Mastery: Intention, Knowledge, Practice, Feedback and Understanding. Understanding is the result of knowledge plus experience.

Hopefully you have had at least one experience of each of the above five secrets. If so, you should have the beginning of understanding (since you have knowledge plus experience). Perhaps you even understand that they were not secrets after all, but you knew them all along.

Make sure you give yourself an exercise today that elevates your understanding of love by personally experiencing one of these tenets of love.

2 more weeks to go!

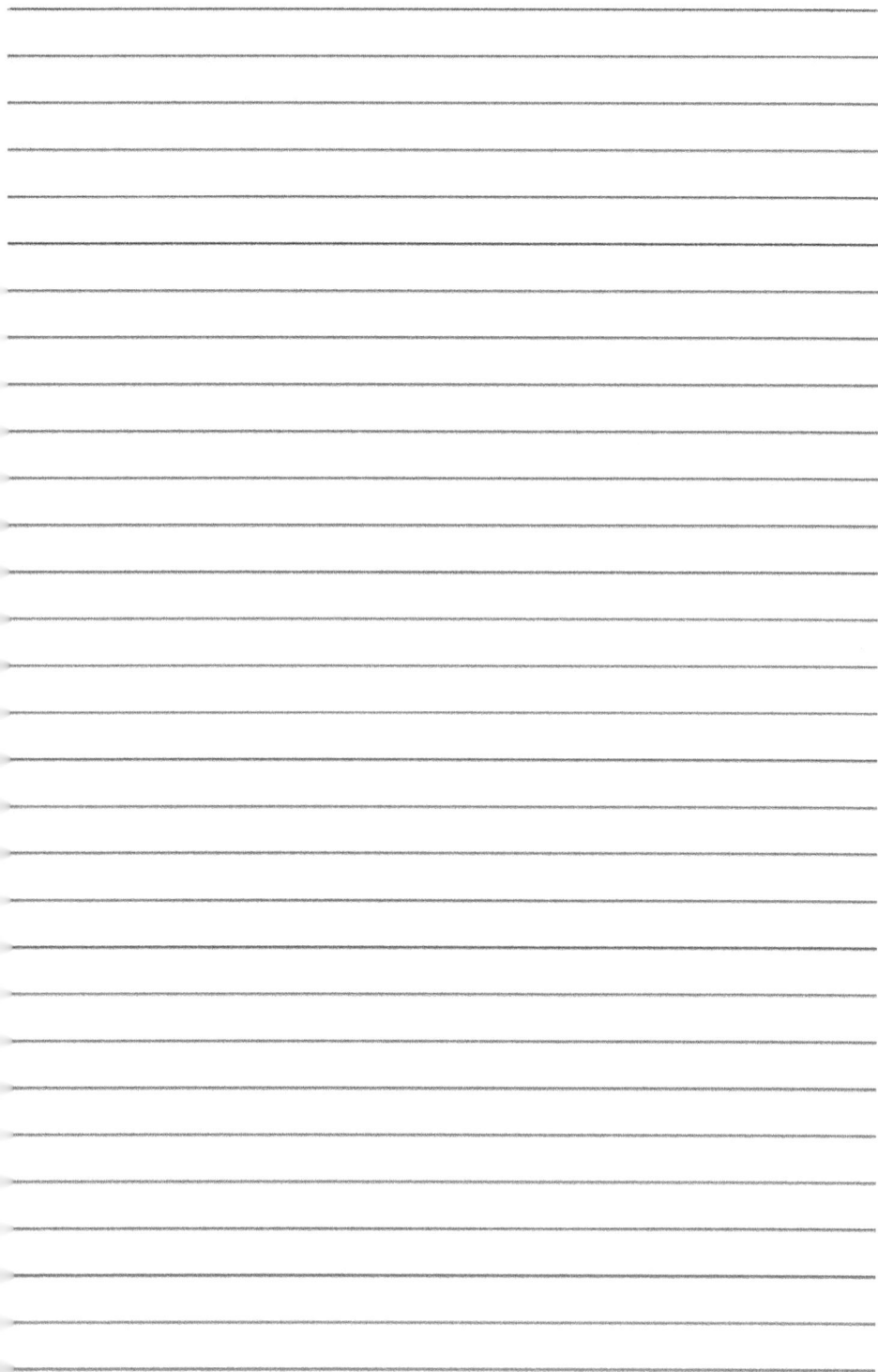

Week 12 - Days 78-84

First Day of the Week:

I AM

Love Exercise Day 78

Look in the mirror for 5 minutes telling yourself with positive enthusiasm, "I am awesome. I am sexy. I am amazing. I am good looking. I am incredible. I am a sight to behold!" Keep going with more effective beliefs.

Journal.

Here's a formula that can change your life:

$$belief + emotion = your\ reality$$

To create the reality you want, give yourself only effective beliefs and put positive emotions behind them such as enthusiasm and love.

The trick for this to work is to be patient, which means to constantly practice this formula and give it time to work. When I started giving myself a new belief about relationships, and did so with enthusiasm, it took ten months before I attracted my romantic partner into my life. But it does not have to take that long. I've heard and read about people who gave themselves a new belief and within two weeks their new reality set in.

Here's an extension of the above formula that can create an amazing result:

If you let go of all of your beliefs, and base all of your emotions on love, your reality will be one of Unconditional Love.

As Scott Peck states in *The Road Less Traveled*, "Life is difficult. Once you truly understand and accept it, then life is no longer difficult."

Accept the above formula, as difficult as it may seem, and life will get easier.

Second Day of the Week:

BODY AND HEALTH

Love Exercise Day 79

Ask yourself, "How can I take care of my body today?"
Spend five minutes letting this question sink into your
subconscious. Feel it in every part of your body.

Journal answers as they come. Take action on those
answers.

Trust your intuition. Listen to your gut feelings, especially when it comes to your health. Know that you have your own answers.

Emotions are primitive thoughts and are products of your nervous system. The nervous system runs throughout your entire body. In fact, your intestines have a tremendous amount of neurotransmitters. Have you ever had a gut feeling? This means that you can hold emotions in your body. Furthermore, when you hold negative emotions, it can cause your body to suffer.

The trick to getting negative emotions out of your body is to let go, relax, and let be. This makes room for new, effective emotions to enter your body. Today's exercise is for you to put a fantastically great emotion into your body that will effectively take care of your body for you.

Here is an adjunct exercise that may help with today's exercise. Imagine yourself in perfect health. What does that feel like? Describe it as well as you can (if you need to, use the emotions chart from Day 67) and write it in your journal. Take these emotions and feel them throughout your body.

Repeat!

_____

_____

_____

_____

_____

_____

_____

_____

_____

_____

_____

_____

_____

_____

_____

_____

_____

Third Day of the Week:

ABUNDANCE

Love Exercise Day 80

Pick another person from your list on Day 66. Contact them and have a conversation about how they can support your dream. If they can support you, ask them what they want and need from you in order to make that happen. Make an agreement.

Journal.

Two people working together in Partnership can be very influential. But three people working together in Partnership can move mountains! Ten people working together in Partnership can change the world!

Today is about expanding your dream team. Whether your dream is to start a business, charity, family, new career, or rise several levels in your job, relationship, income, or health, you will reach it faster with a team of people who want to support you. This will happen if the way they support you is also one of their most important values. Dream teams work best if all partners are being fulfilled.

Balance is one of the Pillars of Partnership (Day 28). I have not talked much about balance, so today is as good a day as any. Having balance within yourself between giving and receiving, as well as leading and supporting, creates one of the four backbone supports of Partnership. Without balance within yourself, or balance between you and your partners, Partnership comes crashing down.

To be out-of-balance is to give all without receiving, and vice versa. The same with all leading and no supporting.

So as you give, receive. And as you lead, support.

As your dream becomes fulfilled in serving others, people serving you will also be fulfilled—if everyone is being authentic to their highest values.

No matter what you want, you can make a dream team around it!

Fourth Day of the Week:

POSITIVE EMOTIONS AND EXPRESSIONS

Love Exercise Day 81

Take 3 people out to a meal. At some point, ask them on a scale from 1-10 how loving you are. Ask them how you can be more loving. Ask for honesty. Be honest with them.

Journal.

Today is about feedback – the 4th step in mastery.

As you do this exercise, keep reminding yourself that intrinsically feedback is neither positive nor negative. It is only positive or negative based upon the meaning you assign to it. So for feedback to be most effective, receive it neutrally without any meaning. Feedback you get from people will reveal if you have been an inspiration to them or not.

Another form of feedback is to look at your results. Did you have a goal around doing *90 Days of Love*? Did you reach this goal? If so, what made the difference? If not, what do you either have to accept or let go of to reach your goal?

Feedback is necessary to become a Master of Love. Don't skip it!

_____
_____
_____
_____
_____
_____
_____
_____
_____
_____
_____
_____
_____
_____
_____
_____
_____
_____
_____
_____
_____
_____
_____

Fifth Day of the Week:

CONNECTION AND GIVING

Love Exercise Day 82

Clean out at least one room in your home and donate all of the stuff you don't want or need to a charity.

Journal optional.

Today is a practice in letting go. But what does this have to do with love?

If you recall from Day 35, I said, "Love is the answer. And you get there by letting go of everything that gets in the way of love. Love has always been inside of you, maybe covered, hidden, or forgotten, but it has always been there."

Is there stuff in your home that is useless to you, yet you still hold onto it? This is because it has value to you. So in order to let it go, you have to think of the greater value that will come in giving it away, such as creating space.

This is the same for your emotions and beliefs. You hold onto them because they have value to you. So instead, think of the greater value of the emotions and beliefs that will replace the old ones. Or possibly the empty space is itself more valuable—for empty space within yourself creates lightness, peace, liberty and freedom.

Lighten Up!

○─○ Sixth Day of the Week:

INNER SELF AND VISION

Love Exercise Day 83

Find a quiet place to sit undisturbed. Relax. Breathe. See how people put up resistance, "walls" and cut themselves off from connection. Visualize all people connected and loving. See all people open. Envision love growing inside all people.

Journal.

On Day 64, there is an exercise on authenticity and increasing your phoniness radar. The more authentic you are, the more you can sense phoniness in others. The same is true for connection. The more connected you become to people, the more you can sense when other people are disconnected.

For those people who do not connect well, imagine them being a castle. What do they have defending their castle? Beliefs, judgments, justifications, blame, anger, regret, guilt, pride, insecurity, ego, envy, shame? There are an infinite number of defenses and weapons that can keep them from connecting with others.

You can boil all of these defenses down to one thing – fear. Beneath all of the defenses and weapons that people harbor is a fear of something. The only cure for fear is faith. Faith is seeing a new possibility for yourself. Faith gives people courage, or the ability to act in the presence of fear.

Today is about interacting with disconnected people. To love someone who fears connection is to allow them to acknowledge and accept their fear. Easier said than done! Start by seeing the world from their perspective, as you practiced on Day 74. Keep asking them questions until you can pinpoint their fear. Perhaps ask them something like this, "What do you think your life would be like if you didn't have that fear?" Support them in finding their faith in living a connected life and encourage them to connect in spite of their fear.

"Encourage rather than discourage." - Joe Luciani, Ph.D.

Seventh Day of the Week:

LOVE FREELY

Love Exercise Day 84

Pick one of the exercises from the past week to do over again. Add your own personal touch, variation or flavor if you wish. Or invent your own love exercise to do today and share it with our community.

Remember to journal!

12 Weeks! Whew! Talk about amazing!

For thousands of years, wise men and women have asked, "What is love?" And for thousands of years, wise men and women have given thousands of different answers. This is because for every person, there may be a different way that they connect with people. Everybody has their own version of love because we can only experience connection from our own perspective.

This is why my answer to the age-old question, "What is Love?" is Love Secret #2, "Love is the emotion of connection." This answer is truly an umbrella statement to cover all possible experiences of connection.

Are there people in your life who may have been attempting to connect with you and you did not realize it because it was outside of your own perspective?

Something to think about!

Week 13 - Days 85-91

First Day of the Week:

I AM

Love Exercise Day 85

Look in a mirror for 5 minutes repeating, "I am loving to everyone. I am loved by everyone."

Journal.

I have found that most people have no problem with the first above affirmation. It is the second affirmation that most people resist. Do you find it difficult to imagine everyone loving you?

The truth is that this second affirmation has nothing to do with whether everyone loves you. It has everything to do with allowing yourself to be loved by everyone. Or in terms of connection, being open to other people's way of connecting. Perhaps it might make more sense if I state these affirmations as follows:

In terms of connection: "I am connecting to everyone. I am connected by everyone."

Or in terms of openness: "I am open for everyone. I am open to everyone."

213

There is always a way to love!

Second Day of the Week:

BODY AND HEALTH

Love Exercise Day 86

Ask yourself, "How do I show love to people?" Spend five minutes letting this question sink into your subconscious. Feel the question in every part of your body.

Journal answers as they come.

Your beingness shows up in your movements, tone of voice, and face. Regardless of any words you may be saying to someone, you are messaging your true self through these other forms of communication. In fact, it is estimated that only 8% of your communication is through words. If you say, "I love you" with a stiff body, melancholy voice and angry face, no one is going to believe you! When your words, movements, vocal tone and facial expressions are all in alignment, you are being authentic. This is because there is not a way to get all of these forms of communication in agreement without your true beingness behind them.

Here's a scary thought. If most people communicate by text – either through messaging, email, memos, twitter, etc., how much of the true communication is getting through?

215

Thus, the best way to show love to someone is in person. The second best way is by video.

Honesty will always get your body in alignment with your words!

Third Day of the Week:

ABUNDANCE

Love Exercise Day 87

Think of your dream. Think of two people you don't know personally who could support your dream. Contact them and begin to create a relationship with them by introducing yourself, or taking them to lunch, or some other way.

Journal.

As you go into these last few days, the exercises will be bigger and take more time. So you may need to schedule them at a later time (but not too much later!) Hopefully you see yourself now as someone who is capable of playing big, especially when it comes to love.

If you don't know someone who could support your dream, start with a web search. But by all means, connect with someone! You are a Master of Love. This is easy for you!

Have fun!

Fourth Day of the Week:

POSITIVE EMOTIONS AND EXPRESSIONS

Love Exercise Day 88

Ask someone out with whom you want to create a relationship. While out, tell them something about yourself that makes you vulnerable. Tell them why you asked them out. Be honest.

Journal.

I have not used the V-word at all up until today—vulnerable. Though I have certainly hinted at it.

Vulnerability means that one is open and revealing. Thus being emotionally vulnerable is a risk. But without opening up your emotions to another person, you cannot create a heart connection.

Because I am asking you to be vulnerable today, make sure you are with someone you want a relationship with. The reason is because emotional vulnerability is one element that will move two people from merely spending time together, into relationship.

Love is worth it.

Fifth Day of the Week:

CONNECTION AND GIVING

Love Exercise Day 89

Make arrangements to volunteer for one full day at a charity, homeless shelter, environmental project, or non-profit of your choice.

Journal Optional.

Today is a day to practice bringing together all of your new knowledge and skills of love. From connecting, to authenticity, being in the NOW, feeling fulfilled, asking people how you can support them, giving unconditionally, loving yourself, vulnerability, acceptance, letting go, appreciation, having fun, abundance, honesty, courage, and a few more aspects of love that I'm sure I had an exercise for!

Wow! Human beings are capable of so much! Why waste it on the small stuff!

Oh yeah, one more thing: Nothing will change your perspective like volunteering for those in need. From me, thank you for being a volunteer.

Big day tomorrow!

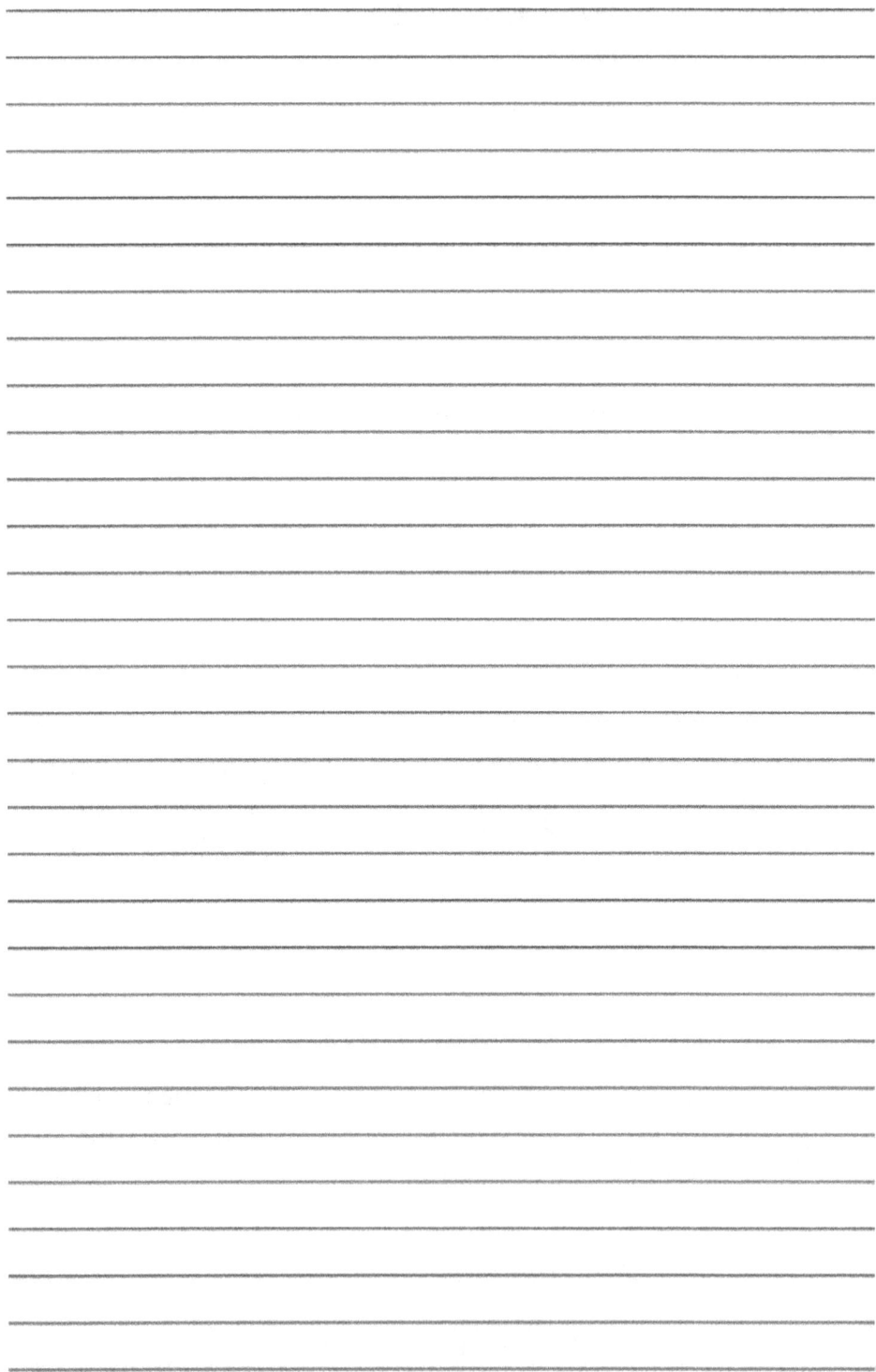

Sixth Day of the Week:

INNER SELF AND VISION

Love Exercise Day 90

Find a quiet place to sit undisturbed. Relax. Breathe. See how love is the emotion of connection. See that the more you are open to love, the more others are open to love.

Journal.

Today, breathe and reflect on this amazing accomplishment and commitment in courage and connection.

I hope you see that love is not one-dimensional. In fact, it is every-dimensional. There is no one-way to love. There are infinite ways. Keep discovering new ways!

Tomorrow, a bonus—Day 91!

_____
_____
_____
_____
_____
_____
_____

♥ Seventh Day of the Week:

LOVE FREELY

Love Exercise Day 91

What do you want to feel today? In your journal, finish the following statement, "I am...." Write as many "I am" statements that come to mind.

Day 91 is the beginning of a new set of 90 days and is a metaphor for the rest of your life. Before you started *90 Days of Love*, your love center was at a certain level. Now, at Day 91, it should be at a higher level. But the truth is that there is no upper limit to love. So though you are at Day 91, it is also Day 1 for the next step in your life, especially in regards to your dream, purpose or mission.

What is next for you? Can you see how you can use love to create the relationships that support you and your dreams? And you support them! That is a mastermind—helping someone while they help you.

So set a new 90 day goal. Or a 1-year, 5-year, 10-year goal. Whatever you do, the most important step in your life will always be the next step.

And Congratulations! I urge you to continue your daily practice to love unconditionally, completely and freely!

Love, Chris

About the Author

Chris Enni is a Partnership Coach, relationship consultant, speaker and facilitator. He is a Certified Partnership Practitioner from the Center for Partnership Studies, and is a Certified Partner with Pax Programs, holding a Professional Certification in Partnership and Empowering Women.

"I learned about a million wrong ways to be in a relationship. As I began to wonder why nothing was working, I was stuck without answers to some essential questions. 'Why do we fight, or even have negative emotions? What purpose are they serving? How can I overcome these negative feelings?' Eventually I realized that I had a rudimentary experience of love. I began to ask myself over and over, 'What is love? How do I create love?' All of the hard work, dedication, discipline and rigor that I put into my career, I poured into learning about love. Through research, trials and errors, and practice, I eventually came up with many exercises that led to my mastery of relationships and love. These results inspired me to create *90 Days of Love*, as well as the Pathway to Partnership courses, so I could lead others, through coaching and by example, into the blissful waters of healthy relationships."

Before Chris became a Partnership Coach, he was a musician in the San Francisco Bay Area. Chris holds a B.A. in music from UCSD and has taught, written and recorded music for many years.

Chris recently spoke at the Transformational Men's Foundation's Get Your Results Seminar in San Diego. He also contributed to the Women's Leadership Development and Wellness Forum in San Diego, as well as to many other organizations and groups.

"One negative thought, emotion or experience is one too many for this short life. Make your life the vibrant, passionate life of your beautiful, big dreams. This is possible through successful relationships, partnership and love."

- Chris Enni

Partnership & Love

Design Your Relationship

Feeling disconnected? Struggling to maintain feelings of love, affection and intimacy? Losing hope for lasting love?

Partnership and Love was founded by Chris Enni and Sarah Galarza as a means to share with the world the simple and effective foundations in creating healthy, respectful and loving relationships. They offer live courses, books, and personal coaching with proven material and exercises in relationship success.

Whether you are single, dating, committed, engaged or married, learn to create long-lasting love and connection with Partnership and Love. Because life was meant to be shared.

To get started on your successful path, go to:

www.partnershipandlove.com

www.ingramcontent.com/pod-product-compliance
Lightning Source LLC
Chambersburg PA
CBHW031510040426
42445CB00009B/168